Contents

Introduction

Writing is the painting of the voice.
                                        Voltaire

Writing Crafts Workshop is a collection of 34 handicraft projects
that either incorporate or encourage kids' creative writing.
Activities range from elegant to eclectic, fun to functional. Some
are easy, others ambitious. And due to this writer's penchant for the
past, many activities are period pieces borrowed from ancient
cultures, the English Medieval and Renaissance periods, the Victorian age, and eighteenth- and nineteenth-century America.

Workshop activities are designed primarily for kids in the inter-
mediate and middle grades, although many projects will also ap-
peal to younger and older writers. They may be used in many ways.
Teachers can incorporate projects in their ongoing writing cur-
riculum; parents can collaborate with their children on projects at
home; and independent-minded kids can undertake projects on
their own with little or no adult supervision. With kids' use of the
book uppermost in mind, the text of each activity addresses young
participants directly.

These projects are more than art projects with a built-in writing
motivation. Introducing each activity is information that provides a
cultural or historical context for the particular craft involved.
Therefore, social studies instructors will find projects such as ancient tablets, Spartan scytales, hornbooks, broadside ballads, and
post card travelogues as relevant to their subjects as to the
language arts classroom. And kids in or out of the classroom will
feel as if they are participating in a living museum.

The activities in the first chapter include directions for making
many essential, and not-so-essential, tools of the trade—desk accessories that would inspire any writer to get down to the business
of writing. Projects range from a portable Victorian lap desk to a
very professional-looking writing portfolio. Chapter Two traces the
development of writing and bookmaking from ancient to modern
times and provides writers with several methods for binding their
own books. Chapter Three features traditional ways to illustrate the
pages of hand-bound books, including directions for constructing a
rolling pin press for block printing. This chapter also features
techniques for creating unusual typography and offers two nonbook formats for putting writing on display. The projects in Chapter
Four explore the science of secret writing. They will make the process of communicating an adventure and will certainly provide
material for many a good mystery or detective story. The last
chapter, "Writing for Fun," is just what the name says. It contains a
number of projects that are mostly for amusement and are designed
to convince writers that writing can be a vehicle for fun and games
as well as a bookish activity.

Interspersed throughout **Writing Crafts Workshop** are Writer's Gallery "exhibits"—features that relate fascinating facts about writers and writing in various historic and cultural periods. At the back of the book is a section entitled "Writing for Profit." It lists book and magazine publishers that are willing to read and perhaps publish writing submitted by kids. Some of these publishers offer nominal payment for the contributions they accept; all of them respond one way or the other with a courteous letter of encouragement. And finally, at the very end of the book, there are eight pages that may be duplicated for personal or classroom use. These pages feature decorative alphabets and graphic devices to use with various projects in the book, and are conveniently cross-referenced within those projects. Teachers and other supervising adults may want to supplement these pages with clip art and transfer type that can be purchased on consumable sheets in any graphic art supply store.

Writing Crafts Workshop has been written and designed as a self-contained workshop, requiring ordinary home and classroom tools and a minimum of store-bought supplies. Below is a list of materials most commonly used in the projects.

acrylic sealer in spray can
bristol board or oaktag
carbon paper
card or cover stock (65- or
    80-pound paper)
carpet tacks
chipboard or poster board
cloth tape
colored felt-tip pens
corrugated cardboard
duplicating masters
fabric
gift wrap
hammer
masking tape
matte knife
nails
oil-base inks or paints

paintbrushes
pencils
plain paper (20-pound bond)
rags
ribbons
rubber cement
ruler
scissors
small jars
sturdy thread
thin cord or yarn
tracing paper
transparent contact paper
turpentine substitute
water-base inks or paints
white glue
wood pieces

1

A Writer's Desk

Whether you're a poet, a short-story writer, a novelist, a playwright, or just a compulsive letter writer, there is nothing more essential than a writing table or desk. And there is nothing more desirable than a desk equipped with beautiful writing accessories. Here's a chapter full of projects to help a writer set up shop in and on a desk. In fact, there's even a project that describes how to make a portable desk—for writers who don't like to travel without one.

Victorian Lap Desk

Victorian ladies and gentlemen liked to have a desk they could carry with them when they traveled or when they merely moved from room to room. That way, whenever the urge to write came on, a desk was available, complete with pen, ink, and paper. Such a portable desk was called a *lap desk* because it was small enough to rest on a lap.

Lap desks were generally made of fine wood, but some were constructed out of papier mâché. Here's a corrugated cardboard version that is sturdy enough to take along in a car or on a train, to a friend's house, or anywhere else an author or letter writer might have a few words to put down on paper.

MATERIALS

Corrugated cardboard box panel, at least 4 feet by 2 feet
Ruler
Pencil
Small jar with lid (for example, a pimento jar or baby food jar)
Matte knife (optional—can use scissors)
Decorative paper, such as gift wrap or nonstick shelf paper, same size as cardboard panel (optional)
Scissors
Rubber cement
Dull knife, such as a butter knife
White glue
Brown packaging tape, 2 inches wide
2 or 3 small boxes (for example, jewelry gift boxes) to hold writing tools and accessories (see step 11)
Quill pen and ink (see Quill Pen, page 7, and Berry Ink, page 9)
Other writing tools and accessories, such as felt-tip pens, pencils, paper clips, erasers, stamps, sponge to blot ink

DIRECTIONS

1. With a ruler and pencil, draw the pattern shown in the diagram onto the corrugated cardboard. The solid lines are cutting lines; the dotted lines are folding lines. Mark the lettered points for later reference.
2. Trace around the bottom of the small jar in the area labeled desk top, where the inkwell will be cut out.
3. Cut out the pattern along the solid lines. Do not cut out the inkwell in the desk top or make the slit in the front end of the desk until you have completed step 4.

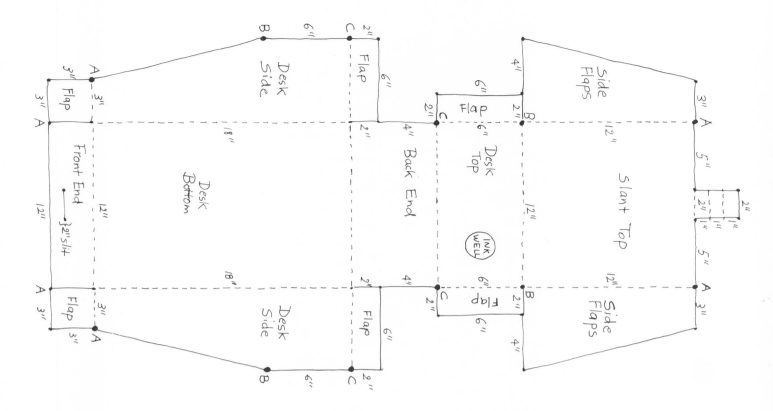

4. If you want to cover the outside of the lap desk with decorative paper, trace the cardboard pattern onto the back of the paper and glue it carefully to the cardboard pattern with rubber cement. (Don't use too much rubber cement or the cardboard will warp.) Then turn the pattern over so that the covered side is facedown. Now cut out the inkwell and make the slit in the front end.

5. Score, or crease, all the folding lines (the dotted lines) with a dull knife. You should be working on the bare cardboard side of the pattern; the side covered with decorative paper should be facedown.

6. Carefully bend all the scored lines upward and in toward the center of the desk two or three times, but not so far that the cardboard threatens to tear.

7. Fold up the desk sides. Turn in the end flaps at all four corners. Lift up the front end so that the lettered point *As* (see illustration) meet at each corner. Use white glue to glue the outside of the end flaps to the inside of the front end as shown. Reinforce the glue with strips of brown packaging tape. (Moisten the adhesive back of the tape so that it sticks.)

8. Lift up the back end to the end flaps that are attached to each desk side so that the lettered point *Cs* meet at each corner. Glue the outside of the end flaps to the inside of the back end as shown. Reinforce the glue with brown tape.

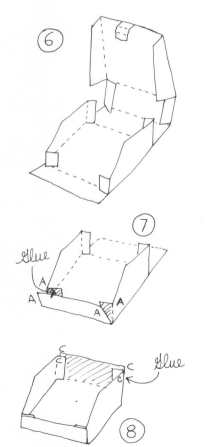

9. Fold in the flaps on either side of the desk top. Lift the desk top over the desk sides so that the top flaps fit inside and the lettered point *B*s and *C*s meet at their respective corners. Glue the outside of the top flaps to the inside of the desk sides as shown. Use brown tape as reinforcement.

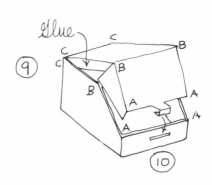

10. Bend up the slant top far enough so that you can fold in the side flaps. Now bring down the slant top to the front end of the desk so that the side flaps fit inside and the lettered point *A*s meet at the corners. To close the desk securely, insert the tab in the slit all the way to the second fold. Withdraw the tab to reopen the desk.

11. Select two or three small boxes that are the right size for the postage stamps and writing tools and accessories you plan to store in the lap desk. Remove the lids or top flaps to these boxes and discard them. Glue the bottoms into position inside the desk.

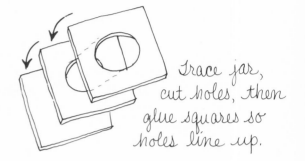

Trace jar, cut holes, then glue squares so holes line up.

12. Cut three pieces of cardboard scrap to 3 square inches each. Trace the small jar two more times on two of these 3-inch squares. Cut out the circles and discard them. Glue the two cardboard squares on top of each other so that the edges of the cutout areas line up. Glue the third piece of cardboard to the bottom of the other two. Then glue this whole construction directly below the hole in the desk top so that edges of the hole and the edges of the cutout areas line up. The jar of ink, when it is not being stored inside the desk, will sit snugly in this inkwell.

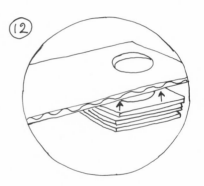

13. Place writing tools and accessories in the box trays inside the desk. Put in a pad or sheets of writing paper. Pour ink into the jar, then close the lid and set the jar of ink in the inkwell. Your desk is ready when you are!

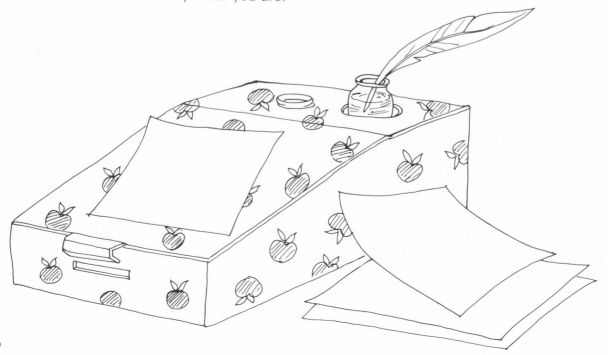

Quill Pen

John Hancock didn't sign his "John Hancock" on the Declaration of Independence so large because he thought himself important. He just wanted King George of England, who was very near-sighted, to be able to read it.

A quill pen might not be as efficient for writing compositions and grocery lists as a ballpoint pen, but it's excellent for signing poems and letters with a real flourish. Therefore, writers who want to sign their "John Hancocks" to a page of some importance—for example, a poem hot off the typewriter—might want to use the same writing instrument that patriots used to sign the Declaration of Independence. And with some practice, a writer can use a quill pen to produce full-length prose and poetry with great beauty and style. After all, it's the same kind of pen that William Shakespeare used to write his plays and sonnets.

MATERIALS

Goose quill or any other good-sized feather with a strong stalk
 (Feathers are available at hobby or craft stores or local poultry farms. A pet shop that sells exotic birds may be willing to save you colorful tail feathers that occasionally drop off the birds.)
Penknife or matte knife
Tweezers or wire
Blotter (see Desk Blotter, page 11) or small piece of sponge and small saucer or jar lid
Ink (see Berry Ink, page 9) or small jar half-filled with water and some food coloring (see step 6 below)
Paper

DIRECTIONS

1. Wash the feather in warm, soapy water and allow it to dry. Then soak the bottom of the quill in hot water for several hours.
2. Use a penknife or matte knife to cut off the end of the quill stalk on an angle as shown in the diagram. This is the pen *nib.*
3. Use a tweezers or a piece of wire to clean out the inside of the quill stalk. Remove the papery pieces of skin very carefully to avoid cracking the nib.
4. Carefully cut a small slit in the pen nib as shown. (This slit will help control the flow of ink according to how much pressure you apply on the pen.) Then cut the very tip of the nib so it's flat.

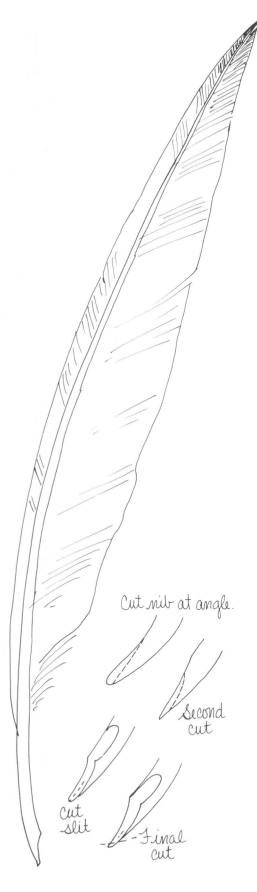

Cut nib at angle.

Second cut

cut slit

Final cut

5. Put a small piece of damp sponge in a saucer or lid of a jar. Or, set down a blotter if you have one or have made one.

6. Open a jar of ink. (Food coloring in a small jar half-filled with water will work also, though not as well.)

7. Dip the nib of the quill pen in the ink. Press the nib gently on your blotter before you begin to write. At first, try writing in a noncursive style, one in which you lift up your pen after each short stroke. Redip the pen in the ink whenever you notice that the ink has become light. Once you think you have the hang of it, experiment by holding the pen at different angles and applying different amounts of pressure. You'll be surprised at the number of variations in the style of a letter that result from *how* you write with a quill pen. When you feel sure of yourself, try your cursive signature.

Note: The art of lettering is called *calligraphy*. The craft project on page 34 provides directions for making an old-style copybook in which to practice calligraphy with a quill pen. For sample calligraphy alphabets, see pages 91 and 92.

Moist sponge for ink blotter

Berry Ink

In colonial days, schoolmasters were usually responsible for making quill pens for their students, but children were expected to bring their own homemade ink to dip the pens in. There were many recipes for making ink. "Lamp black," or soot scraped from the inside of a lamp, mixed with a little water became black ink. Empty nutshells, oak galls, or the bark of trees could be boiled to make brown ink. The juice from ripe berries made red, blue, or purple inks. Or different powders could be purchased and mixed with a little gum and water to make ink. Today most writers buy commercial ink for their pens, but why buy ink when you can make your own?

MATERIALS

1 cup of ripe blueberries, blackberries, boysenberries,
    loganberries, raspberries, strawberries, or black cherries
Strainer
Small bowl
Spoon
1 teaspoon of vinegar
1 teaspoon of salt
Brewed tea (if needed)
Small jar with lid

DIRECTIONS

1. Place a few berries at a time in the strainer. Holding the strainer over the small bowl, crush the berries with the back of the spoon so that the juice drips into the bowl. The skin, seeds, and pulp of the berries will remain in the strainer. Discard them and crush a few more berries, repeating the process until all the berries have been juiced.
2. Add the vinegar and salt to the berry juice and stir until the salt dissolves.
3. If the ink solution is too thick, dilute it with a little tea.
4. If the ink solution is too pale, add a drop of red or blue food coloring.
5. Pour the ink into a small jar. When you are not using the ink, keep the lid on the jar. Unfortunately, berry ink won't last long, so make only a little at a time. When it starts to harden, throw it away.

WORD INVERSIONS: A CALLIGRAPHER'S TRICKS

Can a word read the same upside down as it does right side up? Can it read the same backward and forward without being a palindrome (a word spelled symmetrically—like madam)? Can it read the same through a mirror? Can it hide inside another word that doesn't share a single one of its letters?

Scott Kim is a calligrapher and type designer who can make the impossible possible. He plays with letter shapes as if they are gumby dolls—stretching them this way and that, pulling one way, pushing another, bending one part backward, leaning another forward, straightening out a curve, and curving a straight line. When he is finished, the letters are still recognizable from the original perspective, but suddenly they assume new forms from any other perspective. Scott calls this kind of visual wordplay an inversion, *and he defines an inversion as an "exactly symmetrical design based on a word or name."*

Inversions are very hard to describe, but easy to see. Here are several examples from Scott's book, Inversions: A Catalogue of Calligraphic Cartwheels *(BYTE Books, a division of McGraw-Hill, 1981). Many writers, after they see Scott's inversions, want to try some of their own. Some participants in the Writing Crafts Workshop may be inspired to design personal name inversions for illuminated letters, seals, and autograph albums. But writer beware! Inversions are harder to design than they look.*

Desk Blotter

Some kids are lucky enough to have their own desks. If so, a desk blotter is a good thing to have on top. It can take on ink blots, scribbles, scratches, and graffiti—marks that would otherwise make a desk top an uninviting place to get a clean start on a new writing project. When the blotter itself starts to look too messy, it's easy to remove the old blotter paper and insert a new one. For those writers who are concerned with appearances, desk blotters keep a desk looking very professional.

MATERIALS

Lightweight cardboard, 2 pieces each 7 inches by 14 inches
Fabric or decorative paper, 2 pieces cut to the same size as the lightweight cardboard
Pencil
Scissors
White glue (for fabric) or rubber cement (for paper)
Heavyweight cardboard, 12 inches by 18 inches
Strong paper, 11¾ inches by 17¾ inches for lining sheet
Blotting papers cut to 12 inches by 18 inches (Blotting papers can be purchased in stationery stores. You should be able to get 2 out of a single standard-sized sheet.)

DIRECTIONS

1. Glue the pieces of fabric or decorative paper faceup onto the cardboard pieces. These will be used to make side pockets on the blotter.
2. Lay the pocket pieces covered side down in front of you. Fold in 1 inch on one of the long sides of each piece. Glue down the folds. Then clip ½ inch off the unfolded corners on each pocket piece as shown.
3. The heavyweight cardboard is the blotter board. If it has a good and bad side, set it down with the bad side up.
4. Slide one covered pocket piece, covered side down, under one side of the blotter board. Position it so that it extends 1 inch from the sides of the blotter board. Fold down the extensions and glue them to the back of the blotter board as shown. Do the same with the second pocket piece. This method of making neat corners is called *mitering*.
5. Glue the lining sheet over the back of the blotter board. It should fit ¼ inch short of the edges of the board and cover up the glued down extensions of the side pockets.
6. Turn over the blotter board. Slip a blotter paper inside the side pockets. Use this surface for any doodling, pen testing, and ink blotting you need to do.

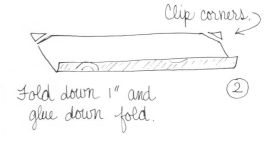

Clip corners.

Fold down 1" and glue down fold.

②

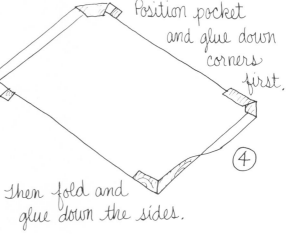

Position pocket and glue down corners first.

Then fold and glue down the sides.

④

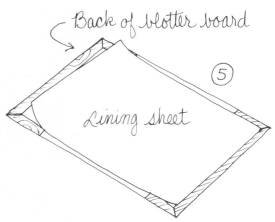

Back of blotter board

⑤

Lining sheet

Slip blotter paper under pockets.

Marbled Pencils

One of the best known pencil makers of all was Henry David Thoreau, the author of *Walden*. In fact, he had a lot more success running his father's nineteenth-century pencil factory than he did writing books. Although most *Workshop* authors and poets don't have to make pencils to support their writing habits, they probably won't want to pass up this classy set.

MATERIALS

Box of pencils, unsharpened
Sandpaper
Marbling solution (see directions on page 22)
Oil base paints for marbling
Turpentine substitute
Sticks for mixing paints
Marbling comb (see directions on page 22) or sticks for
    making patterns in the colors
Masking tape, a narrow width
Drinking glass
Newspaper
Rags
Acrylic sealer in spray can

DIRECTIONS

1. Sand the paint and varnish off each pencil.
2. Prepare the marbling solution. Thin the oil-base paints and apply drops of color on the surface of the solution as directed in steps 2 and 5 on page 23. Use a marbling comb or a stick to swirl the colors into a pattern you like.
3. Wind masking tape around the top of each pencil to cover the metal band and eraser.
4. Hold the ends of the pencil with your thumbs and index fingers. Lay the pencil flat on the surface of the marbling solution and slowly roll it forward until it has picked up marbled colors all over the wood casing.
5. Lift the pencil out of the solution. Carefully rest the bottom on a sheet of newspaper. Remove the masking tape with one hand while balancing the pencil with the other. Then lean the eraser against a glass or jar.
6. You should be able to marble at least four pencils before you need to apply new colors. When you do, first skim the surface of the marbling solution with a strip of newspaper to remove the old colors.
7. Allow the marbling to dry thoroughly—at least two or three days. Then spray on a coat of acrylic sealer so that the marbled colors won't chip or scratch.

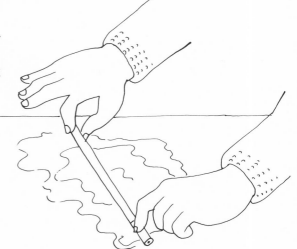

While pencils are drying, make a matching pencil holder. (See page 14.)

PENCILS IN THE PAST

The word pencil comes from the Latin word pencillus, meaning "little tail." It was the name for brushes that medieval scribes used to apply ink on paper. The writing tool we call a pencil came centuries later, but the medieval name stuck.

According to legend, during a storm in 1554 in Borrowdale, Cumberland, England, a large oak tree fell over. Beneath its roots was found a deposit of graphite, which was thought to be a kind of lead. Chunks of graphite were mined to use as marking stones.

The first real pencils were shaped sticks of graphite wound around with string. As a writer needed more lead, the string was unwound. Later, pencils were made as they are today—a mixture of clay and graphite baked and fitted into a wood casing.

Can you guess what was used as the first pencil eraser? Bread crumbs!

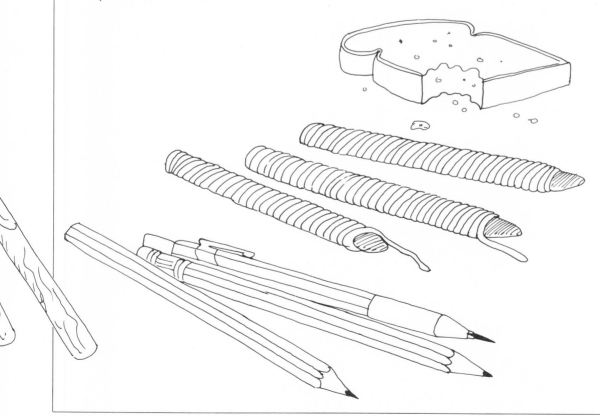

Pencil Holder

In colonial days, children's school accessories included a slate, chalk, and a box to hold their pencils. Even today, many children carry pencil boxes when they first start school. But for those writers who have outgrown the pencil box, here is the pencil holder. It can be made to match a fine set of marbled pencils or a desk blotter; or it can second as a container for other graphic tools, such as a pair of scissors, ruler, matte knife, and pens. No matter how a pencil holder is made or used, a writer's desk is incomplete without one.

MATERIALS

Oatmeal carton or salt cylinder (or any other cylindrical cardboard container 3 to 4 inches in diameter)
Tape measure
Scissors
Marbled paper (see page 22), fabric, or other decorative paper
Rubber cement (for paper)
White glue (for fabric and felt)
Black construction paper 4½ inches wide and long enough to fit around the inside of the cylinder with a little overlap
Felt (about 3 to 4 inches in diameter)

DIRECTIONS

1. Measure 5 inches up from the bottom of the cardboard container and draw a line all around the circumference at this height. Cut along this line and discard the top.
2. Measure the circumference of the container. Cut a piece of cover material (marbled paper, decorative paper, or fabric) that measures 7 inches wide by the length of the circumference plus ½ inch.
3. Fold over ¼ inch of one 7-inch side of the cover material.
4. Lay the cover material facedown. Apply rubber cement or glue all over the outside surface of the container. Place the container at the unfolded end of the cover material so that ½ inch of material extends past the bottom of the container, and 1½ inches of material extend past the top.

Draw a line 5" from the bottom.

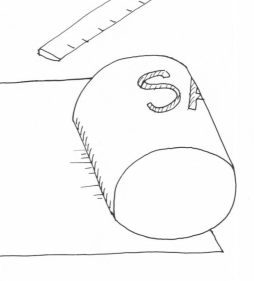

5. Press the unfolded end up against the container and roll the container forward. The cover material will stick to the surface of the container as it makes contact. Add a little extra glue or cement along the inside of the folded end and press it down on the container. The fold should overlap the unfolded end by ¼ inch and make a neat seam.

6. Fold all the excess material over the top of the container, smoothing it down along the inside surface. Then fold over the excess material at the bottom onto the base of the container.

7. Apply glue all over one side of the black construction paper. Carefully insert the paper inside the container so that it rests on the bottom, the gluey side facing the walls of the container.

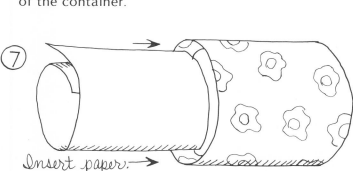

⑦ Insert paper. →

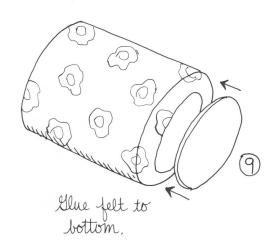

Glue felt to bottom.

⑨

8. Press down one edge of the paper, then move your hand along the inside, pressing the paper against the walls as you do. The paper should fit around the inside with a ½-inch overlap. It will neatly cover the ragged edges of the folded over excess material.

9. Cut a circle out of felt that is about ½ inch less in diameter than the bottom of the container. Glue this felt circle to the outside bottom of the container, centering it carefully so that it fits within ¼ inch of the edge all around. The felt will cover up the ragged edges of the folded over material and will act as a no-scratch surface to rest on the desk.

Illuminated Letters

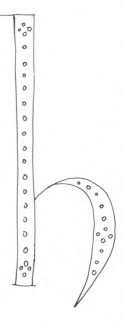

In early medieval times, when a book was truly a *manuscript* (Latin for "handwritten"), there were two people responsible for its production. The first person was a scribe, who wrote out the text. The second was an artist who *illuminated* the manuscript by adding beautiful decorations. These illuminations were splendid and filled with color. Often gold leaf, a foil made from real gold, was pressed into the design to make it glitter.

Illumination became popular again during the sentimental Victorian era. Victorian ladies in particular considered it fashionable to design their own monograms or initials on writing paper. Garlands of roses, sprays of tiny flowers, cherubs, and many golden flourishes adorned these elegant letters. It was also very popular to decorate the outside of a matching envelope with similar illuminations.

Letter writers who are artists as well can put their talents to work creating beautiful personal stationery. But since it takes so much time, illuminated letters ought to be saved for special friends and special occasions.

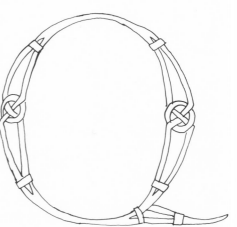

MATERIALS

Plain writing paper and envelopes
Monograms or elegant initials alphabet (duplicate or trace an alphabet on page 89)
Tracing paper cut to the size of the writing paper
Ruler
Pencil
Carbon paper
Watercolor paints
Paintbrush
Gold paint, gold glitter, or gold transfer foil
White glue (optional—for gold glitter)
Black felt-tip pen or quill pen and india ink

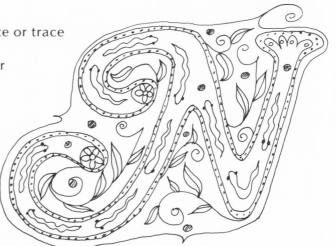

DIRECTIONS

1. Decide where you want the monogram or initials to appear on the writing paper. With a pencil and ruler, draw a straight line at the same place on a sheet of tracing paper (see step 4). This will be the baseline for the monogram or initials. Mark the center point.

2. Position the tracing paper over a monogram or elegant initials alphabet (see page 89) so that the middle letter of the monogram, or your middle initial, appears in the center of the baseline. Trace the letter.

3. Reposition the tracing paper so that the first letter or first initial appears to the left of the middle letter on the baseline and trace again. Then reposition the tracing paper to trace the last letter or initial on the baseline to the right of the middle letter. The monogram or initials will appear in proper sequence and straight on the edge of the baseline.

4. Lay a sheet of carbon paper, carbon side down, on top of a sheet of writing paper. Lay the tracing paper with the monogram or initials on top of the carbon paper. Position the three sheets on top of one another so that the top edges and lefthand corners line up. Retrace the letters of the monogram or initials firmly so that they are transferred by the carbon paper to the sheet of writing paper below.

5. Separate the sheets. Save the tracing paper and carbon paper to make more illuminated letters later on.

6. In light pencil, sketch in the designs and decorations you want to illuminate the monogram or initials. You can also illuminate a border around the sheet of writing paper.

7. Fill in the illumination with watercolors. Use gold paint or glitter to add luster. To make them stand out more, go over the light carbon lines of the letters with a black felt-tip pen or a quill pen dipped in india ink.

8. Don't stop here. Take a matching envelope and make it look as lovely as your writing paper.

Note: You don't have to use monograms or elegant initials on illuminated letters if that's not your style. You can try letters from Variations-on-a-Theme Typography or an Animated Alphabet (see pages 50–51), or use letters from the other alphabets provided in the back of the book on pages 85–92.

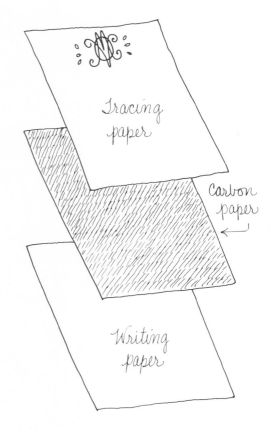

Letter Holder

One of the rewards of being a letter writer is getting letters in return. But sometimes the return mail starts to stack up. In that case, a letter holder comes in very handy.

A letter holder is as easy to make as a pencil holder and as useful for desk top organization. A letter holder is also a handy place to keep phone messages, lists, and other scraps of information that otherwise clutter up a writer's desk.

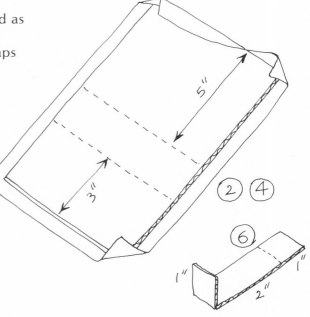

MATERIALS

Corrugated cardboard, 5 inches by 10 inches
Decorative paper, fabric, or other cover material cut to 6 inches by 11 inches (save the scraps)
Rubber cement (for paper) or white glue (for fabric)
Paper, 4½ inches by 9½ inches for a lining sheet
Ruler
Pencil
Dull knife, such as a butter knife
2 corrugated cardboard strips, 1 inch by 4 inches

DIRECTIONS

1. Glue the cover material back to back on the large piece of cardboard so that the material extends ½ inch past the side of the cardboard all around.
2. Fold and glue down the flaps of extra material, mitering the corners as shown on page 11.
3. Glue down the lining sheet so that it covers up the edges of material, leaving a neat ¼ inch of material uncovered all around. If you have leftover scraps of cover material, cover and line the cardboard strips also.
4. With the covered side of the cardboard down, draw a line across the 5-inch width, 3 inches from one end. Draw a parallel line 5 inches from the other end.
5. Score the lines with a dull knife. Then bend up the cardboard at either end along the scored lines until each side sits at a right angle from the flat base. The shorter panel is the front of the holder; the longer panel is the back.
6. Draw a line across each cardboard strip 1 inch from each end. Score the lines and fold them up at right angles.
7. Insert one folded cardboard strip sideways between the front and back panels of the letter holder. Glue the outside surface of each end flap to the inside surface of the front and back panels. Insert the second folded strip in the other side and glue it in the same way. The strips act as braces to hold the front and back panels at right angles to the base. Set letters and messages on top of these braces.

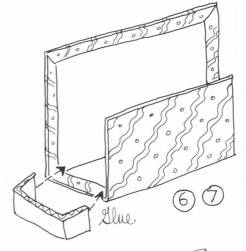

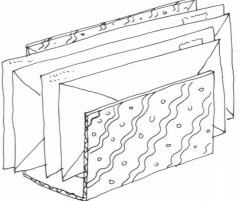

18

Personal Seal

Until 1840, there was no such thing as a gummed envelope. A letter was first folded so that one end would overlap, addressed on the other side, then turned back over again and sealed with wax. While the wax was still warm and soft, a signet, or seal, was pressed into it. In the base of the seal was carved a personal symbol or initials that left a raised impression in the wax. (Both the signet device and the impression it makes are called seals.)

Some stationery today is still made for folding and sealing. It's also proper to add a seal for decoration on an envelope that's already been licked closed. Sometimes colorful stickers are used in place of wax seals. But for that old-fashioned, elegant touch, nothing can replace a personal seal.

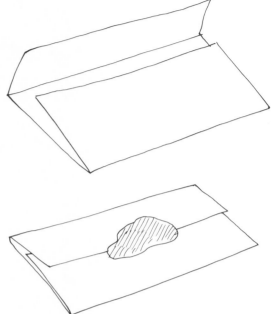

MATERIALS

Small cube of self-hardening clay
Sharpened pencil, toothpick, or other pointed stick for carving in clay
Sandpaper
Acrylic sealer in spray can
Salad oil
Stick of sealing wax (Sticks of sealing wax are available in stationery stores—they're usually sold along with brass signets that have machine-engraved initials for people who haven't the time to design their own.)
Matches
Letter to seal (see Note)
Paper towels

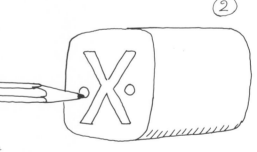

HOW TO MAKE A SEAL

1. Shape the clay into a cube or rectangle with a base at least 1 inch square.
2. Carefully incise the outline of a design with a pointed tool. Make a picture symbol, initials, or a geometric shape—but keep the design simple. (And remember to carve letters backwards.)
3. Carve out the areas around the design that you don't want to print. Cut into the clay base at least ¼ inch deep so that the design really stands out when the outside areas are all cut away. Allow the clay to dry several days.
4. Sand the surface of the design smooth and level after the clay has thoroughly dried and hardened. Spray on several coats of acrylic sealer.

HOW TO USE A SEAL

1. Apply a light coat of oil with a paper towel to the surface of the design on the seal. Be sure to oil all around the raised areas. The oil will prevent the wax from sticking to the clay.

2. Strike the match and then light the end of the wick on the stick of sealing wax. Hold the stick at an angle directly over the spot on the letter paper or envelope where you want to place a seal. The wax will drip onto the spot. The amount of wax you want will depend on the size of the seal.

3. When the splotch of wax is large enough, blow out the flame. Immediately press the carved design into the soft wax. (If you wait too long, the wax will cool and harden, and the seal will not leave an impression that is deep enough to be seen.)

4. Lift the seal and check the impression. If the seal is not quite positioned correctly, or if a portion of the design extended outside the splotch of wax and therefore failed to impress, "erase" the seal by simply dripping more wax on top of it. Then try pressing again.

5. Remember to apply a light coat of oil to the surface of the seal for each use. If the surface is still oily after you have finished, wipe it dry with a clean paper towel.

Note: Seals were also used to authenticate documents, such as contracts, in times past. Every seal was unique, like a fingerprint, so its owner could be identified. If a ruler impressed the royal seal, it was proof that he or she had personally issued the document and considered it to be quite important.

Personal seals can go on an IOU, on a classroom work contract, or on a list of New Year's resolutions. A seal will emphasize the importance of the document and a commitment to what's written inside.

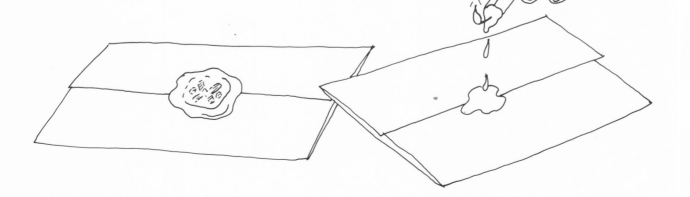

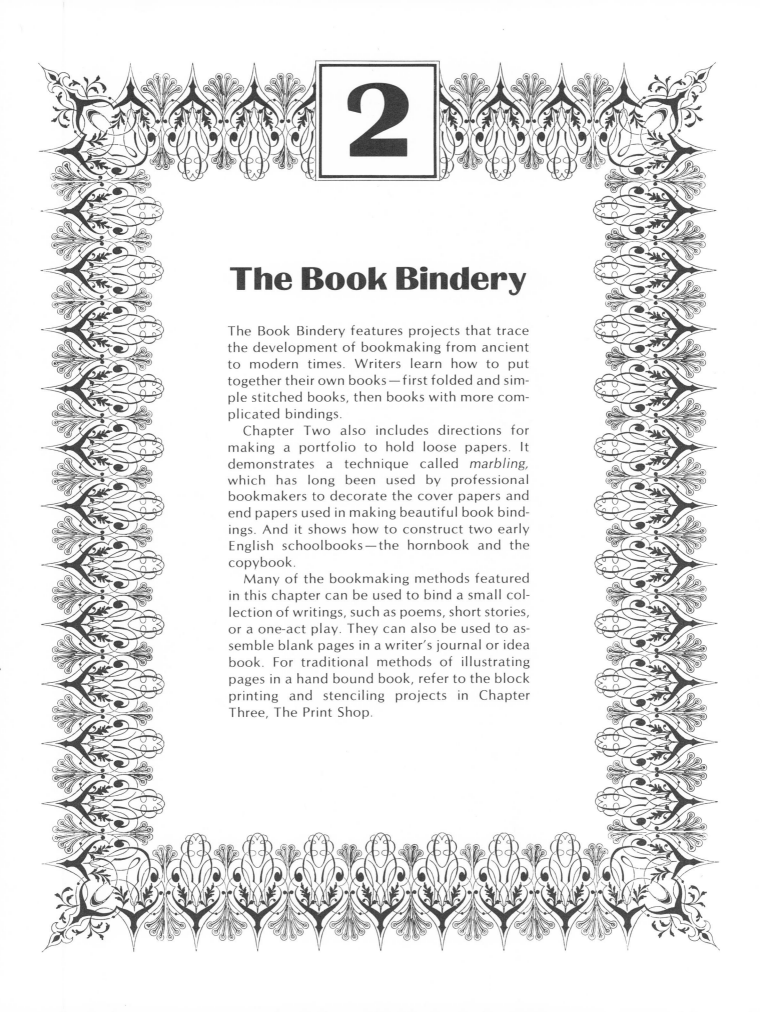

2

The Book Bindery

The Book Bindery features projects that trace the development of bookmaking from ancient to modern times. Writers learn how to put together their own books—first folded and simple stitched books, then books with more complicated bindings.

Chapter Two also includes directions for making a portfolio to hold loose papers. It demonstrates a technique called *marbling,* which has long been used by professional bookmakers to decorate the cover papers and end papers used in making beautiful book bindings. And it shows how to construct two early English schoolbooks—the hornbook and the copybook.

Many of the bookmaking methods featured in this chapter can be used to bind a small collection of writings, such as poems, short stories, or a one-act play. They can also be used to assemble blank pages in a writer's journal or idea book. For traditional methods of illustrating pages in a hand bound book, refer to the block printing and stenciling projects in Chapter Three, The Print Shop.

Marbled Paper

Marbling is the art of floating different patterns of oil-base paints or inks on the surface of water and transferring the patterns to paper. The water is mixed with a thickening substance which allows the colors to sit on the surface without dissolving. This mixture is called *size*. Patterns are usually made by moving the drops of color with a stylus or comb. In Japan, the ancient art of *suminagashi,* or "ink floating," is similar to marbling. Circles of black and indigo ink are dropped on water without size, then the artist blows on the surface of the water so that the colors move in currents to make smokelike patterns.

Marbled papers are used by book binders as end sheets, the pages that go between the covers and the pages of a book. Sometimes the edges of book pages are dipped and marbled, and marbled papers are often used as decorative cover material on the outside of a book. In Japan, suminagashi has been used traditionally as special writing paper for poetry.

Marbled paper is ideal for many projects in Writing Crafts Workshop that require decorative cover material. The same bath of size used to marble paper can also serve to marble pencils (see Marbled Pencils, page 12).

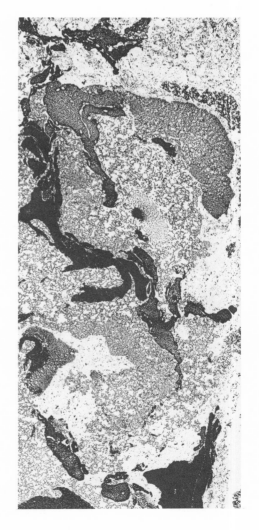

MATERIALS

Large, shallow baking or roasting pan, about 9 inches by 13 inches by 2 inches
1 packet (1 tablespoon) of unflavored gelatin
2 cups very hot (but not boiling) water
2 cups cold water
Spoon for mixing solution
Oil paints or oil-base inks
Paint pots—for example, an old ice tray, a styrofoam egg carton, or several baby food jars
Turpentine substitute (available in hardware and art supply stores)
Sticks for mixing (chopsticks are good)
Paper for marbling (experiment with a variety of white and colored sheets)
Old newspapers

For Marbling Comb (optional):
2 strips of corrugated cardboard, about 2 inches by 8 inches (no longer than the width of the pan you use to hold the size)
Dull knife
15 straight pins
Masking tape, narrow width
Rubber cement or white glue

HOW TO MAKE A MARBLING COMB (optional)

1. Measure and draw lines ½ inch long and ½ inch apart along the long side of one cardboard strip as shown.
2. Score the lines with a dull knife.
3. Press a straight pin into each scored line so that the pointed end extends past the edge of the cardboard (see illustration). Be sure the head of each pin is imbedded in the corrugated cardboard.
4. Cover the row of pins with a strip of masking tape.
5. Glue the second strip of corrugated cardboard on top of the first so that the pins are sandwiched between them.

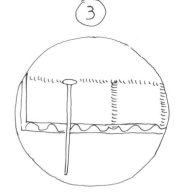

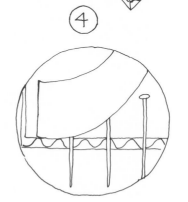

HOW TO MARBLE PAPER

1. Pour the gelatin in the pan. Add the hot water and stir until the gelatin has softened and dissolved. Then add the cold water and stir well. This solution is called *size*.
2. Squeeze about an inch of paint or ink from each tube into a separate pot. Dilute it with turpentine substitute until it is a little runny.
3. Test the colors by flicking a drop of each from a mixing stick onto the surface of the size. The drops should float on the surface, expanding to no more than 1 to 2 inches in diameter. If a drop sinks to the bottom of the pan, dilute the color some more. If it spreads too far or becomes too thin, add more paint or ink to thicken it.
4. Use the edge of a folded sheet of newspaper to skim the test colors off the surface of the size. Now you are ready to marble.
5. To start, flick drops of color from the ends of the mixing sticks onto the surface of the size. Try to drop the colors at regular intervals, about 2 inches apart.
6. Move the colors into patterns with a marbling comb or a toothpick, or blow gently on the surface of the size to create a moving current.
7. When you have a pattern you like, carefully lower a sheet of paper onto the surface of the size. Lower the center first, then the sides so that there are no air bubbles

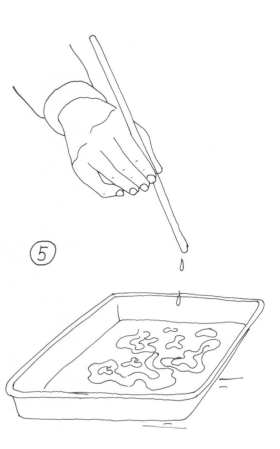

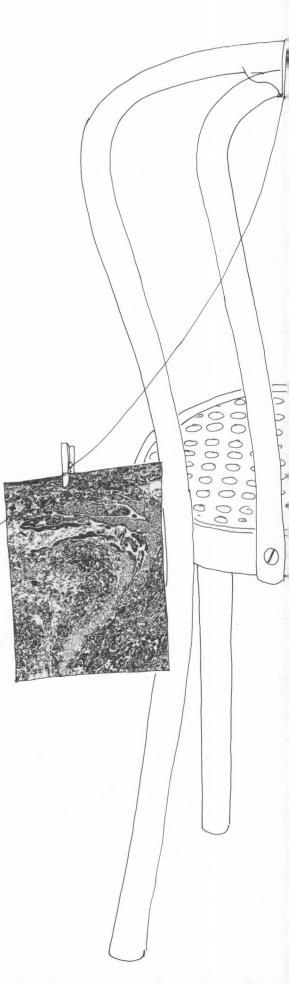

trapped underneath. As soon as the whole sheet has touched the size, lift up one edge and gently pull the paper off the surface. Allow it to drip over the pan a few seconds, then place it faceup on a sheet of newspaper to dry or use the drying line shown here.

8. Skim the surface of the size again with folded newspaper to remove any leftover drops of color and begin again. Experiment with different color combinations, patterns, and papers. For example, spatter colors rather than drop them carefully; or produce a stunning effect by marbling on colored sheets of paper rather than white sheets. Pale pastel colors might appear surprisingly delicate and pretty, while bright colors create a very jazzy effect.

9. After the sheets of marbled paper have dried, they might need pressing. Just leave them flat under a stack of books or other heavy objects for a few days. Then store them in a portfolio (see Writer's Portfolio, page 25) or folder. Marbled papers make lovely writing paper, special gift wrap, and beautiful cover material for books and desk accessories.

HOW TO MAKE A DRYING LINE

1. Tie a line of strong twine or wire between two upright objects; for example, two chairs.
2. Untie one end of the line. String on binder clips through the holes in the metal tops or through the springs of spring-clamp clothespins. Retie the end of the line. Space the clips or clothespins out evenly along the line.

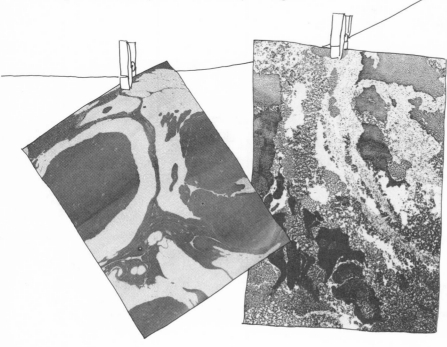

24

Writer's Portfolio

An artist's portfolio is designed to carry prints, photographs, mounted pictures, or paintings. A portfolio can be almost as big as the artist—and very difficult to carry around. Writers are more fortunate in this respect. Chances are, even a writer's greatest masterpiece is typed out on paper no larger than a standard 8½- by 11-inch sheet. Therefore, a writer's portfolio is just the right size for carrying under an arm, in a book bag, or on the back of a bike.

A portfolio makes a professional-looking case for carrying writing assignments to and from school, or an album in which to display loose sheets of creative writing. A portfolio is also a good place in which to keep writing crafts, such as marbled paper, samples of calligraphy, printed playbills, and broadside ballads. In Japan, a portfolio like this one has an entirely different use. It is a carrying case for letter paper and envelopes—in other words, a letter writer's portfolio.

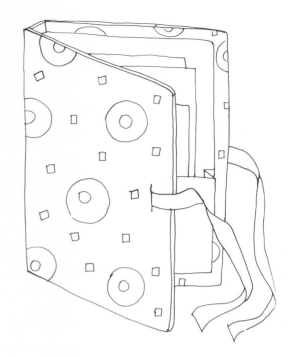

MATERIALS

2 pieces of heavy cardboard, 9 inches by 12 inches each
Heavy cardboard strip, 1 inch by 9 inches
Decorative paper, fabric, or other sturdy cover material,
   13 inches by 20¼ inches
Ruler
Pencil
Rubber cement (for paper) or white glue (for fabric)
Matte knife
2 lengths of ribbon, 6 inches each
2 sheets of lightweight cardboard such as oaktag or bristol
   board, 3½ inches by 10½ inches each
Paper for lining sheet, 11½ inches by 18¾ inches

DIRECTIONS

1. Lay the sheet of cover material facedown. Arrange the pieces of cardboard on top as shown in the diagram. Use a ruler and draw guidelines on the cover material to position the boards accurately. Then spread glue all over one side of each board and press it firmly in place.
2. Fold and glue down the flaps of cover material over the boards, mitering the corners. Press the material down into the ⅛-inch spaces between the spine and cover boards.

Front cover board

Cover material

Spine board

½"

½"

⅛

½"

Back cover board

½"

3. Halfway down the left side of the front cover board, and about 1 inch in, draw a line the width of your ribbon. Do the same on the right side of the back cover board. Use a matte knife to cut slits along these lines. Be sure you have cut all the way through the boards and through the cover material on the outside of them.
4. Insert a ribbon from the outside of the front cover board through the slit to the inside. Glue down 1 inch of ribbon directly on the board. Insert the second ribbon through the back cover board and glue it down.
5. Glue down the lining sheet, centering it so that it covers the edges of the flaps, leaving ¼ inch of material showing all around. As before, be sure to press down in the spaces between the spine and cover boards.

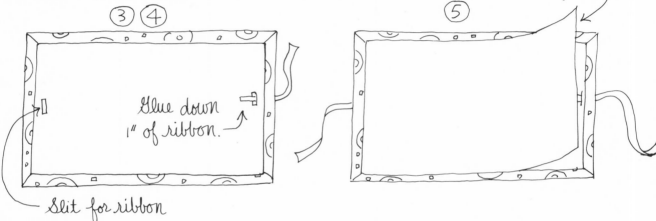

③ ④

Glue down 1" of ribbon.

Slit for ribbon

⑤

Glue down lining sheet.

6. Fold over the front cover, using the space between the cover and spine as a hinge. Then fold over the back cover.
7. Cut the two pieces of lightweight cardboard to the dimensions shown. The solid lines are the cutting lines; the dotted lines are folding lines.
8. Fold up the bottom flaps. Then accordion-fold the side flaps as shown. These are the pockets for the inside of the portfolio.
9. Spread glue on the bottom and outermost flaps of one pocket. Position the pocket on the inside front cover of the portfolio so that the bottom and left side of the pocket line up with the bottom and left side of the lining sheet. Glue the second pocket down the same way so that the bottom and right side of the pocket line up with the bottom and right side of the lining sheet on the inside back cover.

The portfolio is finished. When the glue on the pockets has dried, insert pages of writing, stationery, or whatever else you want in the portfolio. Tie the ribbons in a bow to keep the portfolio closed securely so that nothing will fall out.

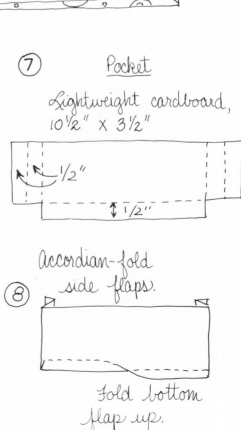

⑦ Pocket

Lightweight cardboard, 10½" X 3½"

½"

½"

⑧ accordian-fold side flaps.

Fold bottom flap up.

Folded Book

The ancient Chinese and Japanese found it difficult to read a scroll—the paper would continually roll up or unroll as they tried to find a place in a long text. It was found that folding up the long scroll into panels of fixed lengths made it much easier to handle. These folded books, *yeh tzu* in Chinese and *orihon* in Japanese, are easy to make and appropriate for displaying a collection of *haiku* or other short poems.

MATERIALS

Long, continuous strip of paper at least 4 inches wide (the one shown here is 6 inches) and 18 inches long (Art supply stores sell individual parent sheets of fine paper from 18 to 35 inches long.)

Scissors

Cardboard or oaktag (2 pieces, about 3½ inches by 6 inches each, see illustration)

Cover material, such as marbled paper (see page 22), gift wrap, or a thin fabric such as cotton in a solid color or print (each piece about ½ inch wider and ½ inch longer than the cardboard)

White glue (for fabric) or rubber cement (for paper)

1 or 2 ribbons, each at least 12 inches long

Pen and ink

Original *haiku* poems or other short poems

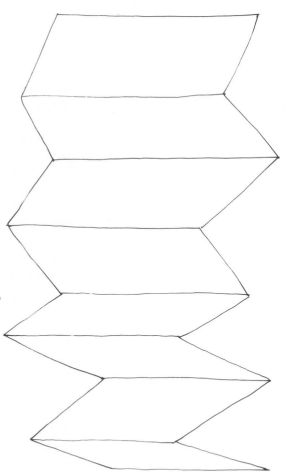

Panels in this example are 3″ x 6″, but this will vary.

DIRECTIONS

1. Accordion-fold the long strip of paper in panels about 3 or 4 inches wide—all panels should be the same width. Trim off any excess paper after the last full panel.

2. Measure the dimensions of one panel. Add ½ inch to each measurement (the width and the length) and cut out two pieces of cardboard to these new dimensions. The cardboard pieces will be ¼ inch larger than the paper panels all around.

3. Add 1 inch to the measurement of the cardboard and cut out two pieces of cover material to these new dimensions. The cover material will be ½ inch larger than the cardboard covers all around.

4. Lay one piece of cover material facedown. Spread glue evenly all over one side of one cover cardboard. Center the gluey side of the cover on the back side of the cover material and press down firmly.

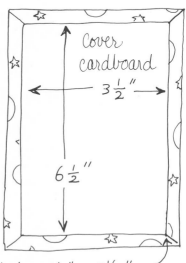

Cover cardboard
3½″
6½″

Cover material, 4½″ x 7½″

5. Glue down the corners of the cover material over the back of the cover as shown. Then fold over and glue down all the edges of the cover material, mitering the corners as shown on page 11.

6. Glue the second cover to the second piece of cover material, mitering the corners.

7. Glue down a piece of ribbon along the inside of the back cover as shown. If you attach one long ribbon this way on the back, it will tie over the front cover to close the book. If you attach a second ribbon on the inside of the front cover as well, the front and back cover ribbons will tie on either side of the book.

8. Spread glue evenly over one end panel of the accordion-folded paper. Press the gluey side down on the inside back cover, centering it. Press down firmly. (The ribbon should extend from under the panel.)

9. Glue the other end panel to the inside front cover following the same procedure. The end panels serve as liners for the insides of the covers, hiding the edges of the glued down cover material and the attached ribbon.

10. In your best calligraphy, write in original *haiku* or other short poems, one on each panel. You might want to reserve the first panel following the liner for a title page. If you have plenty of poems, write one on the back of each panel as well.

11. Decorate a paper label with the title and poet's name, and glue it on the outside of the front cover. Tie the ribbon over the front (or the two ribbons on either side) in a bow.

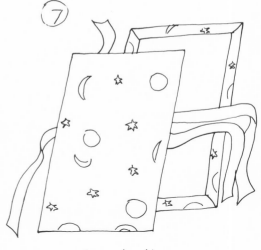

Ties at sides.

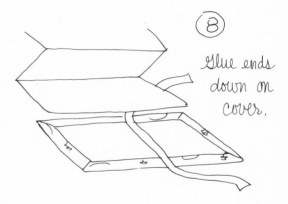

Glue ends down on cover.

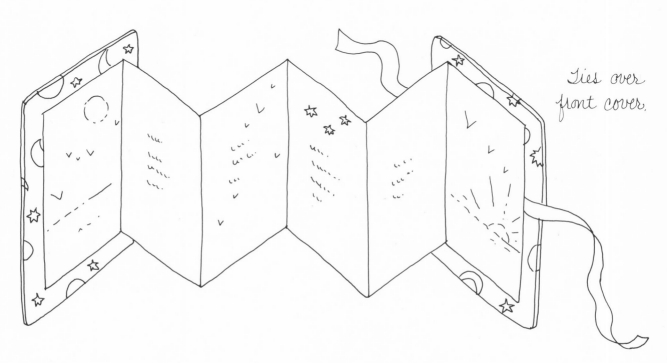

Ties over front cover.

JAPANESE RENGA POETRY

Japanese renga, *or linked verse, is composed as a round robin among a group of poets. It is a chain of* waka *poems— verses written in the syllabic pattern 5-7-5-7-7: the first line has five syllables; the second, seven syllables; and so on. Some writers may recognize the first three lines of* waka *as the familiar pattern for* haiku *poetry.*

Renga were composed by court poets in the twelfth century and continued as a popular tradition until the eighteenth century, giving way after that to the shorter haiku. *Renga were composed in this way: One poet would write the first three lines of 5-7-5; a second poet would write the next two lines of 7-7; a third poet would write another three lines of 5-7-5; and so on. Sometimes as many as a hundred verses would be composed by only four or five poets in one meeting.*

Composing renga *can be a challenging activity for a writing class or a group of writer friends. But it is important that participants first appreciate the Buddhist ideas behind these short poems. Zen Buddhism is a Japanese religion which teaches that through zen, or meditation, a person can experience a deeper awareness. Through that awareness, a person may gain insight or new knowledge about the interconnections between all things in nature. A moment of such insight is what Japanese poets try to recreate in their lines of* renga *and* haiku. *Here is a Japanese* haiku *translated into English as an example:*

> Behold, an old man
> Cutting stalks of pampas grass
> Behind him, the wind.
>
> — *Taniguchi (Yosano) Buson*

In his poem, the poet sees an old man with white hair and bent back cutting stalks of white-plumed grass. When suddenly the wind blows from behind, it causes the grass to bend over like the man. For a brief moment, the form of the man and the bowed grass are the same— heads white and backs weak with age. The poet does not write all this, but uses phrases that suggest these images. The poet writes sparingly so that the reader must experience the moment of deep awareness for him or herself. If this haiku *had been composed for* renga, *the next poets might have contributed these lines:*

> Milk-white grasses drop their seed
> Old ones make way for new ones.

> No room in the house
> Grandfather dies on the day
> My sister is born.

Simple Stitched Book

For a book that is 32 pages or fewer (8 folded sheets), a few stitches can produce an attractive binding. The stitching becomes part of the book's simple but elegant design. A soft cover (paper cover) is sewn in with the pages, but a decorated jacket can be wrapped around the cover to protect it.

In Japan, this easy method has been used for almost a thousand years to bind books of traditional poetry and folktales. Some writers will be inspired by the delicate appearance of such a book to write in poems in their best calligraphy and illustrate the pages with block prints as the Japanese have. Others may want to keep a journal inside. Simple stitched books require very few materials and very little time, so they can be made as needed.

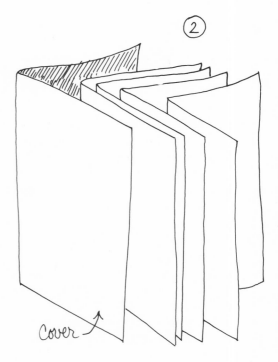

MATERIALS

4 to 8 sheets of paper for book pages
Cover stock (65- or 80-pound) or other heavyweight paper, that measures the width of the book paper by the length of the book paper plus ¼ inch
Sewing needle
Sturdy thread, such as button twist
Scissors
Paper (can also be cover stock), cut to the width of the book paper by the length plus 4¼ inches (optional—for jacket)

DIRECTIONS

1. Fold the sheets of book paper in half.
2. Insert one sheet of folded paper inside the other, until all the sheets are gathered in the middle.
3. On the innermost sheet, mark the middle point on the fold. Then measure an equal distance above and below this mark, say 2 inches, and mark these points as well.
4. Fold the cover paper in half. On the outside fold, mark the same points as you did on the innermost folded sheet in step 3. Then insert the gathered sheets inside the folded cover paper. Jog them so that all the top and bottom edges line up evenly.
5. Thread the needle, but don't knot the thread. Insert the needle down through the middle point on the innermost sheet, pushing through all the folds of the gathered sheets and cover. Pull through all but about 3 inches of thread. Come up through the top point, then back down through the middle point, holding down the little tail of thread dangling on the inside with a finger while pulling the thread taut. Now come up through the bottom point. Slip

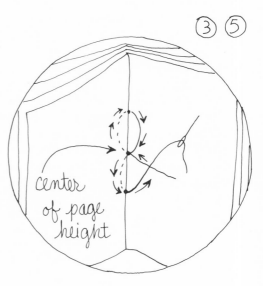

off the needle. Tie the two ends of thread in a tight knot at the middle point. Snip the ends so that they are an even 1 or 2 inches long. (To tie the thread on the outside of the book rather than the inside, begin the stitching by inserting the needle through the middle point on the outside of the cover to the inside of the innermost sheet.)

6. *Optional Jacket:* Fold the jacket paper in half. Measure 2 inches from each end and make two more folds as shown. Then wrap the jacket around the book, folding the end flaps over the sides of the cover.

7. Remove the jacket to decorate it. You can print an illustration directly on it using a rolling pin press (see page 43). For the title and author, use stencils, special effects typography, or your own calligraphy. An alternative is to print all that information on a label and paste it to the jacket. This is especially effective when the jacket is decorated paper, such as gift wrap or marbled sheets. You might also want to write a description of the book and the author on the inside panels of the jacket which fold around the cover. When the jacket is finished, rewrap it around the covers of the book.

Note: If the pages of the book are to be preprinted in any way before binding, you will need to make a *dummy.* A dummy is a model or layout of the inside of a book.

Insert the same number of folded sheets of paper inside one another as in step 1. Staple the gathering on the fold to hold it together. Each folded sheet will make four book pages—two on either side of the fold front and back. But because the sheets are inserted in the middle of one another, the four pages will not necessarily fall in direct sequence. As a matter of fact, only the pages produced by the innermost sheet will fall in sequence. So you must page your dummy to figure out where to print the text so that when the book is bound, the sequence of printed matter will be correct.

Beginning with the outside of the bottommost folded sheet, number each page—on the bottom righthand corner for righthand or *recto* pages, and on the bottom lefthand corner for lefthand or *verso* pages. Paste in copies of the text on the appropriate pages. Then remove the staples, and separate the folded sheets. Follow the layout of each sheet when preprinting the pages of the book. Then, when the real book pages are folded and stitched, the text will fall in proper sequence.

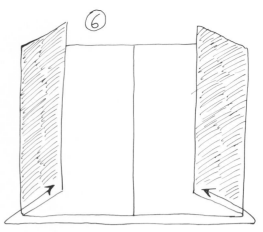

Width of cover plus 4 ¼"

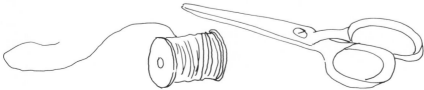

Hornbook

The first schoolbooks used in England and colonial America were hornbooks—and they really weren't books at all. A hornbook was a piece of wood shaped like a Ping-Pong paddle with a printed lesson sheet pasted on one side. A thin layer of transparent horn from a cow, goat, or sheep was tacked over the lesson sheet to protect it. At first, parents or schoolmasters made hornbooks for school children by hand, but later, book publishers had them printed on cardboard paddles.

The lesson sheet on a hornbook usually included the letters of the alphabet, numerals, and the Lord's Prayer. Of course, kids who use the Writing Crafts Workshop already know their *P*s from their *Q*s, but younger brothers and sisters will probably appreciate an old-fashioned gift that helps them learn their *ABC*s. And who said a hornbook has to have an alphabet? What about a multiplication table, or a list of U.S. presidents, or a few easy-to-forget state capitals, or any other set of facts kids need to brush up on?

MATERIALS

Heavy cardboard, at least 6 inches square (the panel of a
    corrugated cardboard box is fine)
Pencil
Ruler
Matte knife or scissors
Short stack of newspapers or magazines
Sheet of white paper
Quill pen and india ink (see Quill Pen, page 7) or a black
    felt-tip pen
Hole punch
White glue
Paintbrush (an old one you had in mind to throw away
    anyway)
Ribbon or yarn, about 6 inches

DIRECTIONS

1. Pencil in two paddle patterns on the cardboard. The measurements are shown in the diagram.
2. Use a matte knife or scissors to cut out the two paddles. If you use a matte knife, work on top of a stack of newspapers or magazines.

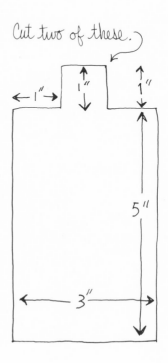

Cut two of these.

3. On one paddle, measure ½ inch in from the edge on all four sides. Pencil in a 2-inch by 4-inch rectangle as shown. Cut out this smaller rectangle to form a window. From now on, this paddle with the window will be called the *frame*.

4. Trace the frame onto a sheet of white paper. Include the window dimensions as well as the outside dimensions, but leave off the handle. Cut along the outside dimensions only. Don't cut out the window.

5. Print a lesson on the white paper. Keep the writing within the inside dimensions of the window. Use black ink for the lesson. To illustrate the lesson, use other colors as well.

6. Glue the lesson page to the paddle. Smooth out any wrinkles or bubbles.

7. Glue the frame directly on top of the paddle so that the lesson sheet shows through the window. Be sure to line up the sides of the paddle and frame all around. Allow the glue to dry.

8. Punch a hole in the bottom center of the handle.

9. Use a paintbrush to distribute a thin layer of white glue evenly over the lesson page. If glue gets onto the top of the frame, wipe it off right away with a paper towel. Allow the glue to dry at least overnight. As the glue dries, it will make a hard, transparent cover that will protect the lesson page. Be patient; it may take a few days before the glue becomes transparent enough so that you can see the lesson through it.

10. Insert the ribbon through the hole in the handle and knot the ends. This strap goes around the wrist or slips on a belt.

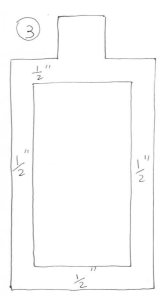

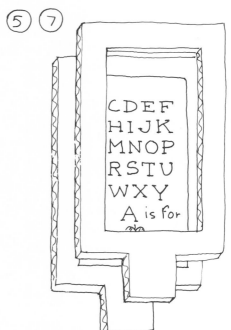

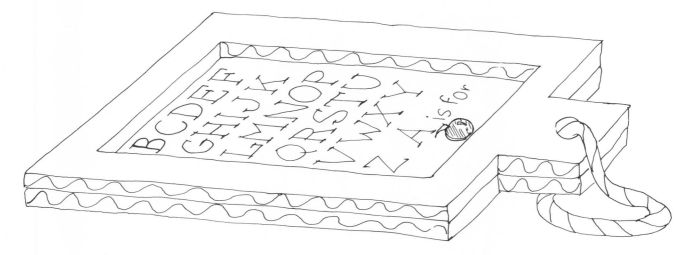

Calligraphy Copybook

In colonial schoolhouses, handwriting was a very important subject—usually the first lesson to follow morning Bible readings. Most often the teacher would provide quill pens, but each child was expected to bring homemade ink and a copybook. The teacher would write a copy lesson into each child's copybook, and the child would copy the lesson carefully many times until the penmanship was perfect.

By the Victorian period, the art of handwriting, or calligraphy, was considered fashionable—a mark of distinction among letter writers. Traveling instructors taught penmanship classes in private homes or in local schoolhouses. Some calligraphers set up shop on street corners to write calling cards with elegant lettering and flourishes.

Today, there are many different *hands* or styles of writing. And practice still makes perfect. That's why calligraphers continue to need copybooks. Here are directions for making a copybook that can be refilled with new ruled sheets after the old ones are used up.

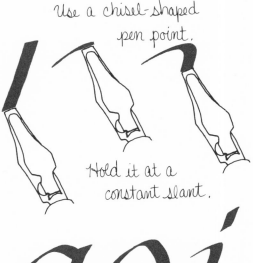

Use a chisel-shaped pen point.

Hold it at a constant slant.

MATERIALS

Lightweight cardboard, such as bristol board, cut to
  8½ inches by 26 inches
Ruler
Pencil
6 sheets of plain, lightweight paper, 8½ inches by 11 inches
Colored pencil
Hole punch
Yarn or cord, about 15 inches

DIRECTIONS

1. Lay down the lightweight cardboard with the 26-inch sides at the top and bottom. Measure 11 inches in from either side and draw vertical lines. Every inch between these two lines, draw another vertical line as shown in the diagram. You should have five lines.
2. Accordion-fold along these vertical lines as shown.

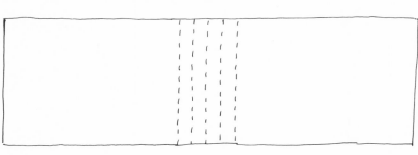

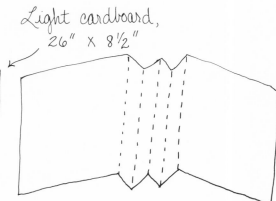

Light cardboard, 26" X 8½"

3. Punch a hole in the center of the first folded cover panel 1 inch from the top as shown. Punch a second hole 1 inch from the bottom.

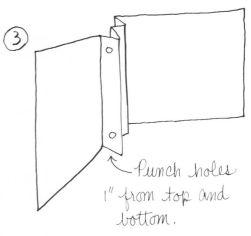

Punch holes 1" from top and bottom.

4. Punch holes in the same positions on the other cover panels. It's easy to do this if you hold the first punched panel against the second panel and punch through the same holes; then do the second against the third, and the third against the fourth. In this way, each punched panel acts as a template for the next.

5. Rule six sheets of plain paper horizontally on front and back with a colored pencil. It's a good idea to make wide rules, about 1 inch apart, to practice letters on a large scale. Rule in dotted lines a little more than halfway above the lower of each set of solid lines to mark the *x height,* or the height of lower case letters such as *x.* Leave extra space between each set of solid lines so that the *descenders* of letters on one line don't run into the *ascenders* of letters on the next line (see illustration).

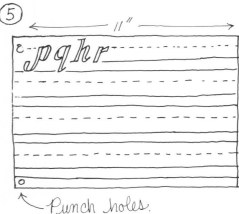

Punch holes.

6. Place one ruled sheet under an accordion-folded panel. Use the panel as a template to trace the punched holes into position on the ruled sheet. Place the sheet on top of two other sheets and punch holes where they are marked. Use one of the punched sheets as a template for the remaining three sheets and punch holes in them.

7. Stack the six ruled sheets so that the holes line up. Insert them in the center of the accordion-folded cover panels as shown. Position them so that the holes in the sheets line up with the holes in the panels. Insert a piece of yarn or cord through the holes starting from the back panel as shown and tie the ends in a bow.

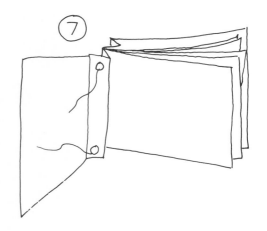

8. To use the copybook, carefully copy in the letters of a calligraphic alphabet, one letter on each set of solid lines. There are sample alphabets on pages 91 and 92. There are also many books on calligraphy available in libraries. If the copybook paper is light enough, it should be possible to trace letters right onto it so that you have a perfect model to copy from. After you have mastered individual letters, try words. Before long, you should be able to write out such things as placecards, illuminated letters, calling cards, poems, and autographs in beautiful calligraphy.

Note: After all the ruled sheets in the book are filled, simply untie the bow, withdraw the cord, remove the sheets, and replace them with new ones.

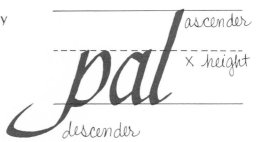

pal ascender

x height

descender

35

Autograph Album

Among the sentimental Victorians, autograph albums were very popular. An autograph album was a record of friendship. It contained personal mementos, such as affectionate poems, locks of hair, silhouettes (shapes cut out of black paper), and sketches. Some homemade albums were quite beautiful, covered in fine-tooled leather or lacquered papier mâché. The pages were decorated with hand-colored borders and flourishes. Printed albums included sentimental pictures and engraved scenes, pretty borders, and short verses by popular Victorian writers.

A friend was expected to sign an autograph book in his or her best handwriting. To be asked to fill an entire page was considered a great honor. Entries were written in charming or witty verse, usually complimenting the owner of the album.

Today, people are a little lazy and usually sign only their names inside autograph albums. But a homemade autograph album deserves more than what you get on a catcher's mitt or a pair of designer jeans. Kids who make fine autograph albums should challenge their friends to come up with witty and wonderful sayings and signatures. One autograph album filled with sentiments from every friend is better than a bunch of birthday cards. It also makes a special keepsake for a friend who has to move away.

MATERIALS

4 pieces of sturdy cardboard cut to these dimensions:
    5½ inches by 7¼ inches (back cover board)
    5½ inches by 1 inch (hinge board)
    5½ inches by 6 inches (front cover board)
2 pieces of solid color denim or other sturdy fabric cut to
    4 inches by 7½ inches each
Ruler
Pencil
Scissors
2 sheets of decorative cover paper, such as marbled paper
    (see page 22), gift wrap, or wallpaper, cut to 6 inches by
    6¼ inches
Rubber cement
2 pieces of paper for lining sheets cut to 6¾ inches by
    5 inches
Cardboard strip, 5½ inches long by 1 inch wide
Hole punch
25 to 50 sheets of plain paper (60- or 70-pound weight is best)
    cut to 5 inches by 7 inches
Heavy yarn—for example, the kind sold for wrapping gifts
Needle with very large eye

DIRECTIONS

1. Trim the pieces of denim as shown in the diagram.
2. Lay one piece of denim facedown with the 4-inch sides at top and bottom. Position the hinge board and the front cover board on top of the denim as shown, leaving ¼ inch between them. Draw pencil lines to mark the positions, then remove the boards.
3. Spread glue on the parts of the hinge board and the cover board that will be glued to the denim. Carefully reposition the boards on top of the denim and press down firmly. Spread glue all over the rest of the denim, fold over the top and bottom flaps, then fold over the side flap. Turn the finished construction over. Press down the denim in the margin between the cover board and hinge board. You should be able to bend up the front cover board along this depression.
4. Position the back cover board on the second piece of denim as shown and mark its position. (The back cover will not have a hinge.) Remove the board and spread glue all over the side of the denim facing up. Reposition the back cover board on the denim and fold over the flaps as you did for the front cover construction.

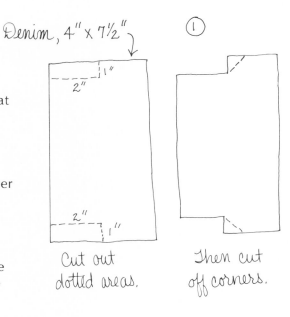

Denim, 4" x 7½"

①

Cut out dotted areas.

Then cut off corners.

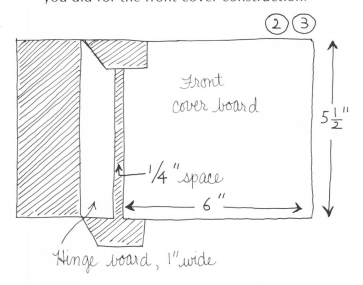

②③

Front cover board

5½"

¼" space

6"

Hinge board, 1" wide

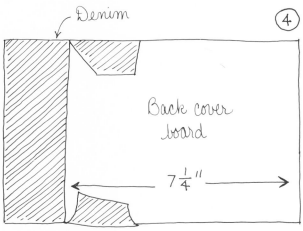

Denim

④

Back cover board

7¼"

⑤

½" of paper extends past cover on 3 sides.

5. Lay one sheet of decorative paper facedown and brush it with rubber cement. Lay the outside of the front cover board down on the paper so that the paper extends ½ inch past the top, bottom, and right side of the cover board as shown. Fold and glue down the flaps, mitering the corners as shown on page 11.
6. Brush rubber cement on the back of one lining sheet and glue it on the inside of the front cover so that it covers the edges of the decorative paper, leaving ¼ inch all around.

7. Cover the back cover as you did the front cover, repeating steps 5 and 6.

8. Make a template out of the strip of cardboard. Starting ⅞ inch from either end punch holes every ¾ inch from top to bottom and ½ inch in from the sides.

9. Line up the templates on the denim-covered side of the front cover (in the hinge board). Punch holes through the template into the front cover. Do the same for the back cover.

10. Snip off ¼ inch from each end of the template. Jog three or four sheets of paper (cut to 5 inches by 7 inches) so that the sides line up. Position the template along one side and punch holes through the template into the sheets. Repeat this step until you have punched holes in all the sheets.

11. Jog all the sheets together so that the holes line up. Place the stack between the front and back covers so that the holes in the sheets line up with the holes in the covers.

12. Thread the needle with the yarn. Follow the diagram carefully to lace up the binding. Then make a knot and snip off the excess yarn. Tuck the ends into the first hole to hide them.

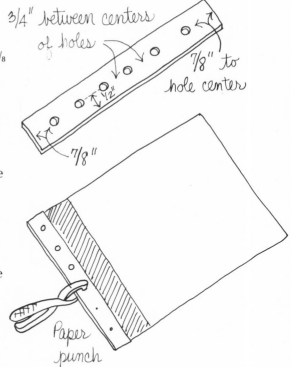

3/4" between centers of holes

7/8" to hole center

1/2"

7/8"

Paper punch

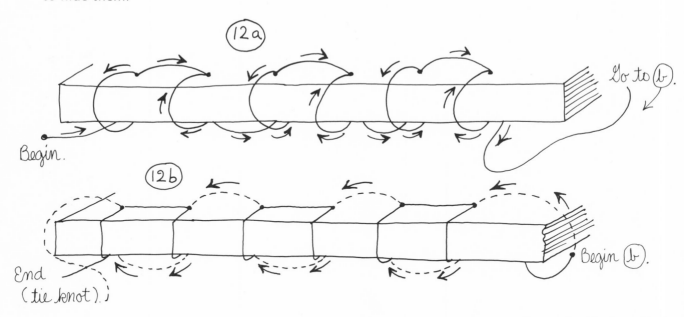

12a

Begin.

Go to (b).

12b

End (tie knot).

Begin (b).

13. Open the autograph album along the front cover hinge. Design a title page on the first page. Some Victorian albums had titles like "Leaves of Affection," "The Jenny Lind Album," "Golden Floral Album," or simply "Autographs." Add a variety of illuminated or hand-colored borders on inside sheets. Then ask friends for their autographs—not just signatures, but original poems and sentiments.

Your finished lacing should look like this.

3

The Print Shop

Some of the projects in this chapter can be used to make the projects in the last chapter more beautiful. Two ancient methods of printing—block printing and stenciling—are introduced as traditional ways for illustrating the covers and pages of handbound books. For the serious book artist, there are directions for making a rolling pin press to use with carved linoleum blocks.

For writers who want to dabble in type design, there are several techniques for creating unusual type for special effects. And finally, The Print Shop features two nonbook publications—the broadside and the playbill. These old-style formats, printed and posted over a century ago, are still effective ways to display writing that demands attention.

Linoleum Block Prints

Block prints were an important step in the development of printing type in both the East and the West. Before movable type was made for a press, the text and illustrations for entire pages of a book were carved on blocks of wood. The blocks were inked, then pressed against paper to transfer the inked images.

Today, block print illustrations are carved into wood or linoleum and printed on a *proof press* like the rolling pin press described on page 43. When a *proof,* or print, of an illustration has been made, it can be pasted up with text type and photocopied or printed on modern equipment. Or a block print can be printed directly on a page for a small edition of books, broadsides, or other writing crafts.

Unfortunately, it's just as easy to cut yourself as a linoleum block. So only people with steady hands and good sense ought to take up block printing. Those who do will find that this type of illustration gives a page of writing the character of old-style printing.

MATERIALS

Tracing paper

Pencil

Carbon paper

Linoleum blocks (available in various sizes from art supply stores)

Set of tools for carving linoleum blocks (sold with linoleum blocks)

Rolling Pin Press (optional—see page 43)

Brayer (hand roller for block printing, available at art supply stores)

Ink plate (pane of glass, formica, or any other smooth surface for rolling out ink—should be twice as wide as the brayer)

Inks for printing (water- or oil-base inks, available at art supply stores)

Paper for printing (Papers that have a large rag content—50% to 100%—are best because they absorb the inks well. Ask a salesperson for help.)

Wood mallet or meat tenderizer (optional—see step 6)

Solvent for oil-base inks (available at hardware and art supply stores)

Rags

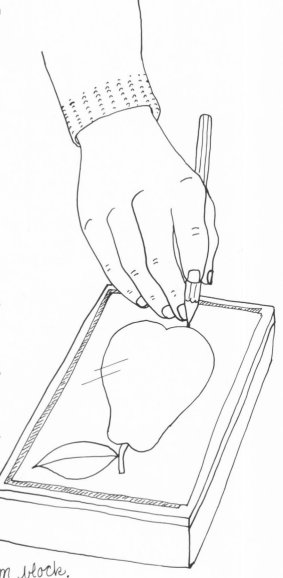

Retrace the backward image so it is transferred through the carbon paper to the linoleum block.

DIRECTIONS

1. Draw an illustration or design on the tracing paper. It should be small enough to fit on the surface of the linoleum block. The artwork should be made up of bold, simple lines and shapes.

2. Turn the illustration over. Place a piece of carbon paper cut to the size of the linoleum block carbon side down on the linoleum surface. Lay the tracing paper illustration facedown on top of the carbon paper. With your pencil, retrace the backward image on the tracing paper firmly so that it is transferred by the carbon paper to the linoleum below. Don't worry that the art now appears in reverse or backwards; when you print, it will reverse itself again.

3. You can cut out the lines of the illustration so that everything but the lines will print; in other words, your design will appear as white lines on a solid color background. Or you can cut away all the areas around and between the lines of the illustration—in this case, only the lines of your design will print in whatever color ink you use. The second method is harder. Use the various size cutting tools to cut away what you don't want to print. *Always cut away from yourself, holding the handle of the cutting tool very firmly.*

4. If you have made a rolling pin press, follow the directions for locking up and printing on pages 44–45. If not, follow the procedure given here in steps 5 through 7.

5. Squeeze out about a teaspoonful of ink onto the ink plate. Roll the ink out evenly with the brayer. Then, roll an even coat of ink on top of your linoleum cut.

6. Position the inked block facedown on a sheet of printing paper. Use a wooden mallet or meat tenderizer to rap the back of the cut several times in several places. Then, holding the paper down with one hand, lift the block straight up off the sheet in one quick movement. If you don't have a mallet or tenderizer, follow this alternate procedure: Lay a sheet of plain paper on top of the inked linoleum block, positioning it as best you can. Press down on the paper with your fingers, and continue pressing out toward the edges of the block so that the paper makes contact with all the inked areas you want to print. Then, take hold of one corner of the paper and peel it off the block carefully. The illustration will appear in reverse from the way it appears on the block itself, but will appear in the same perspective as did your original drawing. Now that you've made your first print, make another!

7. When you have finished printing, hang your prints on a drying line like the one shown on page 24. Use a wet rag to remove any ink left on the surface of the linoleum block and the brayer. If you have printed with oil-base ink, soak the rag in solvent instead of water to clean it.

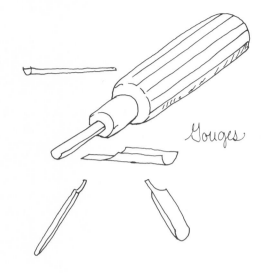

Gouges

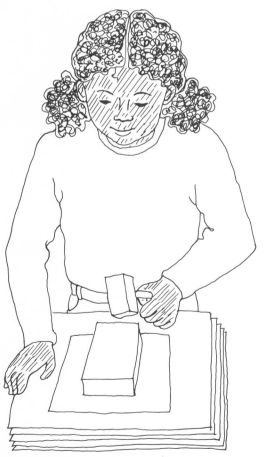

Place a padding of papers under the printing paper.

EMPRESS SHOTOKU'S MILLION PRINTED CHARMS

The Empress Shotoku of Japan was a very devout Buddhist. After eight years of civil war had come to an end during her rule, the empress made and carried out a religious vow. She ordered the construction of one million tiny wooden pagodas. Each pagoda was four and one-half inches high and three and one-half inches wide at the base. Inside each pagoda was placed a tiny roll of paper. The roll of paper had printed on it one of four charms, or sayings of Buddha, that were believed to have magical powers. When the pagodas were completed, they were distributed among ten temples.

Why are Empress Shotoku's million charms so important? The printing of these charms sometime between the years 764 and 770 is the first record we have of printing from wooden blocks. And although western culture considers the invention of printing to have occurred with the invention of movable type, in both the East and the West block printing was the important forerunner. In fact, printers in the East continued to print with blocks long after movable type was invented. With their more than 40,000 ideographs, or symbols, compared to our 26 letter alphabet, the Chinese and Japanese found that movable type wasn't worth the trouble it took to make and set by hand.

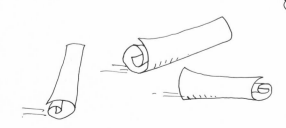

Rolling Pin Press

Imagine what it was like before printing. It was the difference between the Middle Ages and modern times. Before printing, the spread of ideas and information came about very slowly, and sometimes not at all. Often, it was the result of conquests rather than peaceful exchange. Even then, many ideas remained locked away in small, private libraries of manuscripts and block-printed books that only a few people had access to. But since 1456, when Johann Gutenberg cast pieces of movable type and put them in a printing press, printing has dramatically affected our ability to spread words to millions of people thousands of miles apart. It has influenced politics, revolutionized science, created social change, and made literature and learning available to anybody and everybody.

Unfortunately, crafting movable type involves a lot of time and skill, more than is practical for a writer's personal needs. But it is possible to make a very simple press for printing illustrations on the covers and inside pages of handbound books, broadsides, and other paper crafts. This kind of press is called a proof press. It is designed to hold carved linoleum blocks (see page 40) or old printer's woodcuts for those lucky enough to find them.

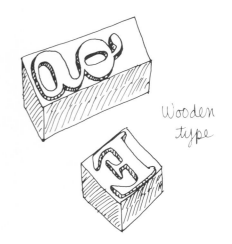

Wooden type

MATERIALS

2 pieces of wood, 1 inch by 1 inch by 10 inches
2 pieces of wood, 1 inch by 1 inch by 12 inches
Plywood or particle board, ½ inch by 10 inches by 14 inches
Glue for wood
Hammer
8 nails, each 1 or 1¼ inches long
Chipboard or poster board, 8 inches by 12 inches
Wood scraps, no more than ¾ inch thick (lengths and widths can vary)
Wooden wedges (see diagram for cutting)
Carved linoleum blocks (see page 40)
Inks for printing (water- or oil-base inks, available at art supply stores)
Brayer (hand roller for block printing, available at art supply stores)
Ink plate (pane of glass, formica, or any other smooth surface for rolling out ink—should be twice as wide as the brayer)
Paper for printing
Scrap paper, several sheets the size of the printing paper
Kitchen rolling pin, at least 8 inches long (preferably the kind with a roller that spins freely on the handles)
Rags
Solvent for oil-base inks (available at hardware stores)

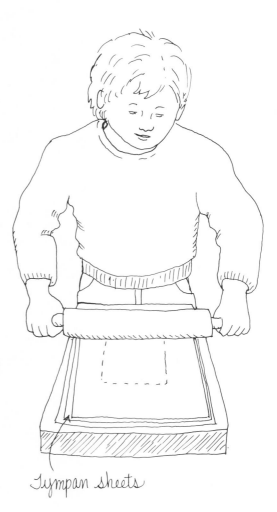

Tympan sheets

HOW TO MAKE THE PRESS

1. Glue down the four pieces of wood (the two 1-inch by 1-inch by 10-inch pieces and the two 1-inch by 1-inch by 12-inch pieces) on the piece of plywood or particle board as shown. Allow the glue to dry.

2. Turn the construction upside down. Hammer a nail down through the plywood base ½ inch in from each corner. Hammer in another four nails along the long sides of the base, each 1 inch from the left or right of the corner nails (see illustration). Be sure to sink the nail heads well into the wood so that the base will lie flat when it is turned back on its right side.

3. Turn the construction right side up again. The inside dimensions of the press box should measure 8 inches by 12 inches. This area is called the *bed* of the press. Lay the 8-inch by 12-inch chipboard in the bed of the press. You may need to trim the sides a bit so that the board fits in easily.

4. Cut up scraps of ¾ inch thick wood to various widths and lengths (illustration shows how wood pieces fit into bed). These pieces are called *furniture.* They will be used to fill in the spaces around your carved linoleum block, or *cut,* when you *lock up* the cut in the press bed so that it won't move as you print. They are a little lower than the height of a mounted linoleum block (which is ⅞ inch high) so they will not pick up ink when you ink the cut.

5. Make two sets of wooden wedges as shown in the illustration. These wedges are called *quoins.* Quoins are used to press the furniture tightly against the linoleum block when you lock up.

HOW TO LOCK UP

1. Set pieces of furniture in the bed of the press along two adjacent sides until you have blocked out the area in which you want to set your linoleum cut.

2. Block in the remaining two sides of the cut with furniture. But on each of these sides, include a set of quoins as part of your blocking. Note that the quoins should be placed between pieces of furniture. They should not rest against the sides of the press itself. You do not have to fill the entire bed with furniture. You only have to use enough so that the furniture will press against the cut on all four sides when you tighten the quoins.

3. Stop inserting pieces of furniture when you have a loose but close fit. Push the wedges of the quoins into one another (see illustration) until they have taken up the slack in the furniture and feel snug. Don't push too hard.

4. Try to jostle the cut. If it doesn't move, you have successfully locked up your cut and are ready to print.

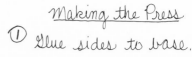

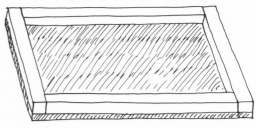

Making the Press
① Glue sides to base.

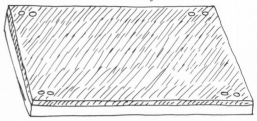

② Nail down through bottom.

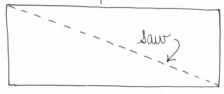

⑤ Wood scrap

saw

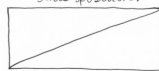

Locking Up

Insert quoins in ② this position.

Push wedges toward one another to tighten.

③

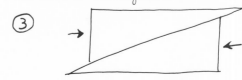

HOW TO "MAKE READY" AND PRINT

1. Squeeze some ink onto the ink plate and roll it out with the brayer.

2. Ink the cut carefully. Make sure all the printing areas have an even coating.

3. First take a press proof. Lay a sheet of printing paper directly on the inked cut. Lay several scrap sheets over the printing sheet. These sheets are the *tympan* sheets and are used as padding. Roll the rolling pin firmly along the sides of the press, starting at one far end. Remove the tympan sheets, then carefully peel the printing paper off the cut.

4. If the print is too light, try again, using additional tympan sheets. If the printing is inconsistent (some areas lighter than others even after you have added more tympan), check to be sure that neither the printing paper or the tympan paper is lying over one side of the press and not the other. If it is, reposition it so it lies between the sides or over both sides.

5. Decide where you want the illustration to appear on the sheet of printing paper. The easiest way to do this is to cut out the illustration in your first proof and glue it in position on a fresh sheet of printing paper. Measure from the illustration out to the top and one side of the paper. Then measure out the same distances from the top and corresponding side of the locked-up cut and make small pencil marks on the furniture to use as paper guides. As you position each sheet of printing paper over the inked cut, try to position it by eye along these marks. If the illustrations aren't quite right every time, they'll be very close.

6. When you have a proof that is evenly printed and positioned where you want it on the page, you are finished "making ready" on the press and ready to print. First, reink the cut. Use the paper guides to position a fresh sheet of printing paper over the cut, then lay the right number of tympan sheets on top. Roll the rolling pin along the press sides and remove your new print. Repeat this procedure until you have the number of prints you want.

7. Hang the prints on a drying line like the one shown on page 24. Use a wet rag to remove any ink left on the surface of the linoleum cut and the roller of the brayer. If you have used an oil-base ink, soak the rag with solvent rather than water.

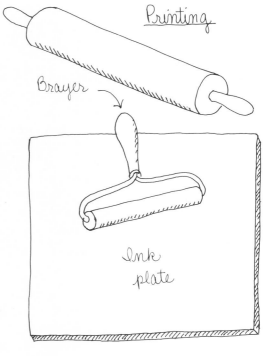

Printing

Brayer

Ink plate

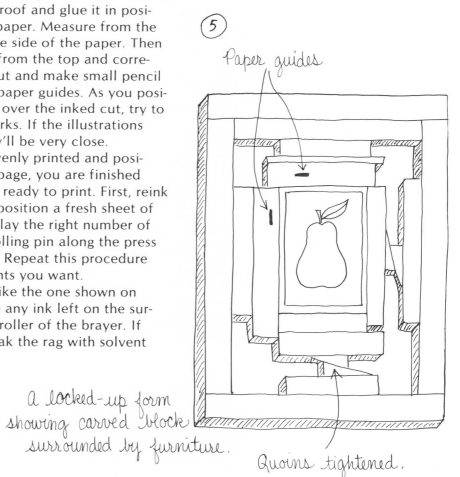

⑤

Paper guides

a locked-up form showing carved block surrounded by furniture.

Quoins tightened.

Paper Stencils

Stenciling has been an early method for duplicating art in many cultures around the world. Chinese paper stencils date back over a thousand years. Chinese stencil designs were first drawn with brushes and ink, then the lines were pricked with a needle. Color was applied through the holes to paper, silk, or plastered walls. Similarly, natives of the Fiji Islands perforated designs in banana leaves to stencil cloth, and Native Americans bit them through paper thin sheets of birch bark to make patterns for beading and quill work. In England and colonial America, cutout stencils were used to decorate walls, furniture, curtains, floors, and so forth.

Stenciling is still one of the easiest ways to duplicate art, and has a long tradition as a method for illustrating the covers or inside pages of handbound books. A simple method for making stencil prints is described here.

MATERIALS

Lightweight cardboard, such as oaktag or bristol board
Pencil
Matte knife
Old cutting board, a stack of newspapers or magazines, or
    some other surface you don't mind scratching
Acrylic sealer in spray can
Paper for printing
Masking tape
Poster paints
Large artist's paintbrush with stiff bristles that round off at
    the ends
Sponge

DIRECTIONS

1. Draw a simple design or picture on the sheet of lightweight cardboard. Fatten the lines that separate the different parts of the design so that they are at least 1/8 inch wide. These are the *ties,* or bridges that will hold the stencil together (see illustration). The other areas of the design will be cut away. Shade in the areas to be cut away with your pencil.
2. Use a matte knife to cut out the shaded areas of your design. Work on top of a cutting board or another surface that you don't mind scratching.
3. When all the shaded areas have been cut out, spray both sides of the stencil with acrylic sealer. The sealer will waterproof the stencil so that it can be cleaned and used more than once.

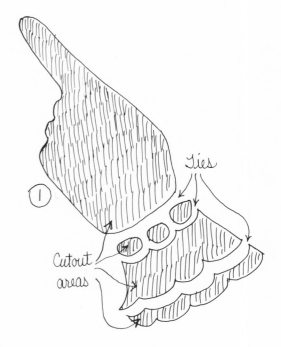

Ties

Cutout areas

4. Set a sheet of printing paper down in front of you. Position the stencil over the paper so that the design falls where you want it to on the printing sheet. You can use strips of masking tape to secure both the paper and the stencil on your work surface.

5. Dip the brush in the paint. On a sheet of newspaper, blot the paintbrush in short dabs so that the paint distributes itself evenly in the bristles. When the brush is coated but not dripping with paint, use the same dabbing motions to paint through the cutout areas of the stencil. This method of painting is called *stippling*. Continue stippling until all the cutout areas are painted solid.

6. Repeat steps 4 and 5 for each stencil print you want to make. When you are finished, set the prints out to dry or hang them on a drying line like the one shown on page 24. Remove excess paint from the stencil with a water-dampened sponge, then rinse out the sponge.

Note: You can use paper stencils to print on cloth, painted furniture, and walls just as colonial Americans did. Use acrylic, enamel, or oil-base paints for this kind of stenciling. Instead of spraying the stencil with acrylic sealer, rub it with a mixture of 50 percent heat-treated linseed oil, called *stand oil,* and 50 percent turpentine before brushing on the paint. Use turpentine rather than water to clean up.

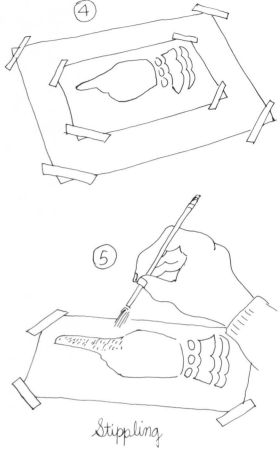

Stippling

Special Effects Typography

For a word or message to have *more* than the impact of a telegram, it will need something zanier than lines, curves, and cross strokes. While you can't very well do away with the alphabet altogether, you can make it a lot more exciting. Here are three approaches to redesigning type so that it explodes, droops, giggles, or stands on its head—or does whatever else a creative typographer wants it to do.

Behind-the-Scenes Typography

It has often been said that the background scenes Leonardo da Vinci's apprentices painted on his Mona Lisa are as beautiful as the Mona Lisa herself. Here is an opportunity for a writer to demonstrate how, with a little background theme and color, a word can become a work of art. Behind-the-scenes typography is the art of filling in the windowlike spaces in letters of a stencil alphabet. The result is a new and extraordinary alphabet, and some very scenic words. It's an especially effective way to highlight the title of a poem, short story, or other descriptive pieces of writing.

MATERIALS

Neatly typed or calligraphed poem or other descriptive writing with 2-inch margin left at the top of the first page for the title (Leave more space for a two-line title.)
Ruler
Pencil
Tracing paper or lightweight white paper (same size as the page containing the writing)
Stencil alphabet (Duplicate or trace the alphabet on page 87.)
Carbon paper
Plain paper (same size sheet as the page containing the writing)
Matte knife
Scissors

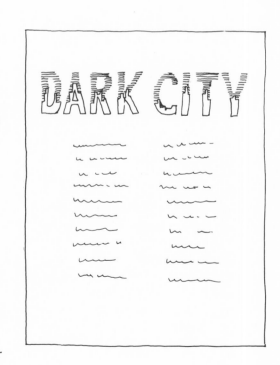

DIRECTIONS

1. With a pencil and ruler, lightly draw a straight line across the top (within the 2-inch top margin) of the first page of writing. This will be the baseline for the letters in the title. (For long titles you may need two baselines.) Lay the sheet of tracing paper over the page of writing and trace the baseline so that it is in the same place on the tracing paper as on the page.

2. Position the tracing paper over the stencil alphabet so that the first letter of the title appears where the title begins on the baseline. Trace the letter. Reposition the tracing paper over the second letter so that it appears on the baseline next to the first letter and trace again. Continue until all the letters of the title appear in proper sequence and straight on the edge of the baseline.

3. Lay a sheet of carbon paper carbon side down on top of the page of writing. Lay the tracing paper with the title on top of the carbon paper. Position the three sheets on top of one another so that all four corners line up. Retrace the letters of the title firmly so that they are transferred by the carbon paper to the page of writing below.

4. The title should now appear in place on the page of writing. Use a matte knife to carefully cut out the letters. When you have finished, erase the baseline you had penciled in earlier.

5. Place the plain sheet of paper underneath the title page. Position the two so that the corners line up. Make a small pencil mark through the bottom of one letter in the title onto the plain sheet. Separate the two sheets.

6. Measure another ½ inch below the mark on the plain sheet and draw a line across the page. Cut along this line and discard the bottom of the page.

7. Color in the scene that is to appear in the title. Choose a design that in some way illustrates the theme of the title. For example, if the title is "On a Rainbow Melting," you might paint horizontal ribbons of each color of the rainbow across the sheet. If the title of an essay is "Dark City," you might draw a repeating pattern of skyscrapers across the sheet. For a poem entitled "The Mane of a Dandelion," you might fill the sheet with bright yellow shaggy flowers.

8. Brush on a thin layer of rubber cement around the edges of the background scene. Glue it faceup behind the cutout title so that the artwork appears through the windows of the stencil letters.

Note: You don't have to be an artist to create wonderful behind-the-scenes typography. Instead of coloring or painting on the background sheet, try gluing on a piece of gift wrap, a colorful cutout from a magazine, or a scene from a black-and-white photograph. Use a colored rather than a plain sheet of paper, and glue on a piece of white lace or fishnet for a textured effect. Use a piece of marbled paper (see page 22) or make vegetable prints (these are like linoleum block prints, but are cut out of vegetables, instead). There are endless possibilities.

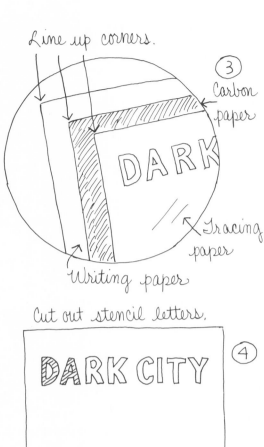

Line up corners.

③ Carbon paper

Tracing paper

Writing paper

Cut out stencil letters.

④

⑥ ⑦

Glue background faceup behind cutout letters on title page.

Variations-on-a-Theme Typography

If you want the word *cold* to look cold, the obvious solution is to make each letter drip with icicles. How hot is *hot*? The steam rising out of each flaming letter should persuade most readers to back off. Here's another way to make every word look like what it means.

MATERIALS

An alphabet (There are several alphabets on pages 85–92 you can duplicate or trace.)

First page of descriptive writing with a 2-inch margin left at the top for the title

Ruler

Pencil

Tracing paper

Carbon paper

Colored felt-tip pens or watercolor paints and a paintbrush

DIRECTIONS

1. Follow steps 1 through 3 in the directions for making Behind-the-Scenes Typography.
2. Now illustrate each letter of a key word so the word takes on some visual characteristics of what it actually means. Use the traced letters as outside guidelines. You may, in fact, need to erase parts in order to add details of your design. For example, for a poem about the "Weapons of a Cactus," you might give each letter in the word *cactus* a headdress of cactus arms with their menacing points. You can illustrate just the key word, or the other words of the title as well.

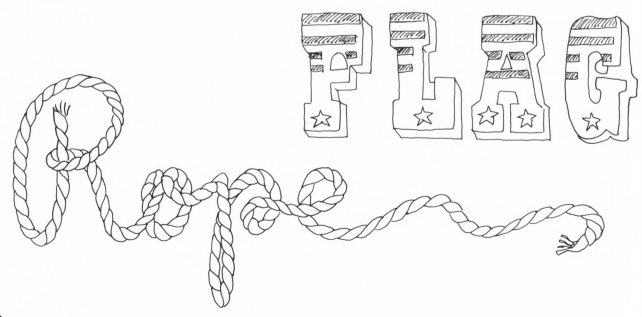

Animated Alphabet

There are few people who have ever looked at a Q without expecting its tail to wag. And a Y has always seemed like a comfortable enough place to snuggle up in with a good book. Here's a way to make letters come alive in a world of their own. Transform an ordinary alphabet into 26 individual characters with personality and movement. Use them for illuminated letters, for initial capitals to begin a poem or a book chapter, or as personal initials on stationery.

MATERIALS

An alphabet (There are several alphabets on pages 85–92 you can duplicate or trace.)
Pencil
Colored felt-tip pens or watercolor paints and a paintbrush

DIRECTIONS

1. With a pencil, draw the characters or details for each letter, letting the form or shape of the letter suggest live features. If possible, decorate all the letters on a single theme. For example, if the theme is "Alphabet Zippers," have each letter appear either zipping or zipped. To create "Alphabirds," draw in the features of different birds until an aviary full of perchers, nesters, and letters on the wing emerges. Try an "Elfabet" or "Letter Ladders" or "Acrobetics" or "Alpharobots" or anything else with movable parts or crazy characters.
2. Color in the letter art.
3. Hang up the animated alphabet as a poster, or use it to create exciting initials and illuminations.

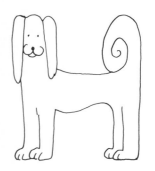

Broadside Ballad

A broadside is a sheet of paper printed on one side. During England's Renaissance, and on through the nineteenth century, broadsides were a popular form of literature sold for pennies on the street. Like newspapers, they recorded the interesting and important events of the time.

Broadside subjects included religion, politics, news, scandals, mystical signs and wonders, advertisements, folk tales, folk songs, and new songs. But even the most newslike topics were often written in verse, as ballads to be sung to familiar folk tunes. Titles and captions of broadside ballads read like newspaper headlines but introduced a text of poetry like the one shown at the right.

Broadsides were always designed to attract attention. Printers used typefaces that were big and bold for the title, then a somewhat smaller type for subtitles and captions. Ordinary type was used for the text, but fancy rules, ornaments, and woodblock illustrations were added as decorations. In general, broadsides looked very busy and a little thrown together.

Today, songwriters can design jazzy broadsides to present the lyrics of their new songs so that friends can sing along. Other writers might revive the broadside ballad to celebrate a special occasion—a "Birthday Broadside"; mark an event— "Ballad of the Coming Comet"; make an important announcement—"Song for a New Sister"; or just state in poetry what's on their minds.

MATERIALS

Plain paper (optional if you use a ditto master; see Note)
Typewriter
Ruler
Pencil
Tracing paper
Carbon paper
Old-style alphabets (Duplicate or trace the alphabets provided on pages 85 and 86.)
Printers' devices and dingbats (Duplicate or trace the old-style ornaments on page 88.)

Job Weeden, Salem News-Boy,

Begs Leave to prefent the following Lines to the GENTLEMEN and LADIES to whom he carries the Effex Gazette.

Jan. 1, 1772.

NOW happily dawns the Year --- Scventy-two.--
Accept my Regards--they're chearful and true.

Pray grant me a Smile---*a little Cafh too.*

No Heat nor no Cold my Courfe does retard:
Your Service is all I ever regard.
Shall I not meet with an ample Reward ?

To pleafe and amufe you---ftill I will go,
As patient as *Job*---blow high or blow low.
Tho' drenched with Rain, or fmother'd in Snow.

Your Goodnefs is great---my Boldnefs excufe,
'Tis not for Beggars to have what they chufe ;
But pray remember, *'tis Job brings the News.*

Courtesy, American Antiquarian Society.

DIRECTIONS

1. Type out the text of the ballad on the sheet of plain paper, leaving room above it for a title and caption. You can also leave room for a large initial capital for the first letter of the first word, a block-printed illustration, or printer's devices, such as decorative rules or borders and *dingbats*. (A dingbat is a typographic ornament used to call attention to something in the text.)

2. With a pencil and ruler, draw straight lines across the top of your typed sheet to use as baselines for the lettering of a title and caption. If you have left room for a large initial capital to start the first line of your ballad, pencil in a short line where you want that letter to sit as well.

3. Follow steps 1 through 3 in Behind-the-Scenes Typography on pages 48 and 49 to trace and transfer the letters of the title, caption, and initial capital. Use the same procedure to trace and transfer decorative rules or borders, and dingbats.

4. Everything should now appear in place on the broadside. Erase all the baselines you had penciled in earlier.

5. Fill in the large letters of the title with a black felt-tip pen, or use colors. Then hang up the broadside ballad where people can see it.

Note: These directions are for creating a single broadside. If you want to produce a large number of broadsides, there are easy ways to go about it. You can produce the whole design on a ditto master (tracing the old-style letters onto the master, rather than a sheet of paper), then run off copies on a mimeograph machine. Or you can photocopy a finished broadside as many times as you like. To use more than one color, you'll have to hand color the broadsides individually with paints or felt-tip pens after they have been run off or copied. You can also print illustrations using paper stencils or using linoleum blocks on a rolling pin press.

Second, pencil in baselines.

First, type in text of ballad.

Ditto master method

A. Remove tissue paper.

B. Write on top sheet, pressing firmly.

C. After writing separate sheets, discard bottom sheet.

BROADSIDES OF THE AMERICAN REVOLUTION

Soon after the colonists declared their independence at a meeting of the Continental Congress in 1776, the Declaration of Independence, written by Thomas Jefferson, was ordered printed and circulated as a broadside. Altogether, there were 19 separate broadside printings of this famous document. A copy written by a scribe was eventually signed by all members of the Continental Congress.

The Declaration of Independence was only one in a series of broadsides which had generated excitement, anger, and strong feelings of freedom in the American colonies before the Revolutionary War began in 1776. The broadside had become the vehicle for public debate on the issues and events leading up to the war. Sometimes both sides of an argument would appear in broadsides on the same day—one side issuing a broadside stating its opinion, the other side responding in a second broadside. These printed news sheets were posted on the doors of meetinghouses and taverns where passersby could read them and react.

One of the more dramatic broadsides of this period featured an engraving by Paul Revere of the Boston Massacre in 1770. Following this were revolutionary broadsides celebrating the Boston Tea Party in 1773; relating accounts of the Lexington-Concord and Bunker Hill battles in 1775; and, in general, protesting tyranny by the British. The British printed their own broadside proclamations and protests on the same issues and events, but from the opposing viewpoint. Together, the broadsides published from 1770 to 1776 retell the dramatic history of events and recall the revolutionary sentiments that resulted in a broadside call to arms.

It has often been said that printing is responsible for lighting the sparks of revolution in ideas and governments throughout the world. Our own American Revolution is an example of how the printing press helped make history.

Glorious Intelligence!

NORWICH, OCTOBER 26, 1781.
Friday Evening, Six o'Clock.
By a Gentleman this Moment from New-London we are favoured with the following Hand-Bill.

NEWPORT, OCTOBER 25.

YESTERDAY afternoon arrived in this harbour, Capt. Lovat, of the schooner Adventure, from York-River in Chesapeake-Bay, (which he left the 20th inst.) and brought us the glorious news of the surrender of Lord Cornwallis and his army prisoners of war to the allied army under the command of our illustrious General, and the French fleet under the command of his Excellency the Count de Grasse.

A cessation of arms took place on Thursday the 18th inst. in consequence of proposals from Lord Cornwallis for a capitulation.----His Lordship proposed a cessation of twenty-four hours, but two only were granted by his Excellency Gen. Washington. The articles were compleated the same day, and the next day the allied army took possession of York-Town.

By this glorious conquest Nine Thousand of the enemy, including seamen, fell into our hands, with an immense quantity of warlik stores, a forty gun ship, a frigate, an armed vessel and about One Hundred Sail of Transports.

NORWICH:
Printed by JOHN TRUMBULL.

Old-Style Playbills

During the English Renaissance and into the nineteenth century, companies of dramatic players, minstrels, and circus performers traveled throughout England's towns and villages. They performed wherever they found room—in barns, weaving lofts, and inn yards. The more popular companies built portable theater booths called *fit-ups* which they carried with them to London's great fairs.

To announce the opening of a new theater production, a company printed colorful broadsides giving the details of the program. These programs were called *playbills*. Some playbills were put up as posters; others were passed out as handbills (today we call them flyers) to passersby. But somehow, today's flyer lacks the pizzazz of an old-style playbill printed with a variety of old typefaces, printers' devices, and woodcuts.

Like theater companies of the past, a student drama group may find that old-style playbills can be one way of attracting a large audience. It shouldn't matter whether the performance is a popular musical or a one-act drama written by a student playwright. If there's plenty of playbill publicity, you can expect the house to be packed on opening night.

MATERIALS

Plain paper (optional if you use a ditto master; see Note)
Ruler
Pencil
Tracing paper
Carbon paper
Old-style alphabets (Duplicate or trace the alphabets provided on pages 85 and 86; for additional alphabets, purchase transfer type such as Letraset from a graphic arts supply store, or create your own.)
Decorative rules and border (Duplicate or trace the rules and borders provided on page 90.)
Black felt-tip pen
Poster paints and a paintbrush or colored felt-tip pens

DIRECTIONS

1. Write out a list of the information you want to include on the playbills. Put all main lines of information in capital letters as shown.
2. Assemble old-style alphabets to use for the lettering of all the main lines of the playbill. Choose a variety of styles and sizes. If you need more than you have, create your own alphabets, or purchase sheets of transfer type.

Middle School Playhouse presents

MYSTERY AT WILLOW POND

the thrilling adventure of detective Star Tabott

played by the incomparable

JESSICA FRENCH

and her two assistants, Mike Shadow & Doctor Smoke,
  by the talented

CARLOS PEREZ & MALCOM RHODES

and also appearing in the superstar cast

RON DAVIES, LISA FRANK, TOBY KAYE, MIKE O'CONNOR,
  KATIE MILARDO.

Written and directed by Middle School's own

DANIEL GOLDSTEIN

Three Grand Performances scheduled for

FRIDAY, SATURDAY, & SUNDAY, OCTOBER 1-3

7 PM to 9 PM

MUSIC AT INTERMISSION

provided by members of the Chorus

TICKETS $1 APIECE

on sale in the lunchroom or at the door

3. On a sheet of paper, lay out the design of your playbill in pencil, drawing in straight lines to indicate the baseline for each main line of type.

4. Follow steps 1 through 3 in Behind-the-Scenes Typography on pages 48 and 49 to trace and transfer the outlines of the letters of each main line of type. *Don't fill in the letters you wrote.* Use the same procedure to trace and transfer decorative rules or borders. If you are using transfer type purchased from a graphic arts store, skip these steps and apply the letters directly on the sheet of paper marked with baselines. Follow the directions that come with the type.

5. The main lines of type should now appear in place on the playbill. Next, carefully handprint the in-between lines of text. When you have finished, erase all the baselines you had penciled in earlier.

6. Color in the main lines of type with poster paint or felt-tip pens. When the colors are dry, the playbill is ready to hang up in a place where a lot of people will see it.

Note: For large numbers of playbills, make photocopies of the original playbill before painting or coloring in the letters. Or produce the original on a ditto master (tracing and transferring the old-style letters onto the master, rather than a sheet of paper), then run off as many copies as you want on a mimeograph machine. After the playbills have been run off or photocopied, color them individually or leave them black-and-white.

MIDDLE SCHOOL PLAYHOUSE PRESENTS

MYSTERY AT
WILLOW POND

the thrilling adventure of detective Star Tabott
played by the incomparable

JESSICA FRENCH

and her two assistants, Mike Shadow & Doctor Smoke
by the talented

CARLOS PEREZ & MALCOLM RHODES

and also appearing in the superstar cast

Secret Writing

The science of secret writing is called *cryptography,* which comes from two Greek words meaning "hidden writing." Whenever people have needed to communicate top secret messages, they have put those messages into *ciphers,* or codes, known only to the people they want to receive the message. If someone intercepts a message sent in cipher, it makes no sense until the code is broken or *deciphered.* People who are in the business of making and breaking codes and ciphers are called *cryptographers.*

Secret writing has been used by many different kinds of people for very different reasons. Military forces use it to signal troops and spies use it to transmit information about enemy activities. It has been a way for prisoners to plan escapes and for gangsters to stage crimes. Poets have used it to hide meanings in their poems, and mystery writers have left cipher clues in their stories. For example, in "The Gold Bug," Edgar Allan Poe uses invisible ink, a substitute letter code, and riddles in a treasure map cipher. In "The Adventure of the Dancing Men," Arthur Conan Doyle's detective, Sherlock Holmes, deciphers a code in which little figures of dancing men are symbols for letters in the secret communications of the underworld.

For whatever reason it is used, cryptography can be a creative challenge for writers with a sense of secrecy or adventure.

A M H E R E A B E S L A N E Y

Spartan Scytales

One of the oldest known devices for communicating secret messages in writing is the *scytale*. Spartan generals exchanged information using twin cylinders and strips of parchment. The sender would wind the parchment around his cylinder, or scytale, and inscribe a message in several horizontal lines. When he unwound the ribbon, the letters of the message appeared out of sequence. Only the person who had a matching cylinder was able to rewind the parchment and restore the original sequence of letters.

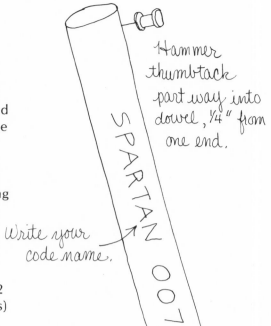

Hammer thumbtack part way into dowel, ¼" from one end.

Write your code name.

MATERIALS

2 pieces of dowel, each ¾ or 1 inch in diameter and 10 to 12 inches long (or 2 pieces of broomstick cut to equal lengths)
2 thumbtacks
Ribbons or paper strips, ¼ to ½ inch wide, cut to 2-foot lengths
Felt-tip pen

HOW TO MAKE THE SCYTALES

1. Gently hammer a tack part way into one of the cylinders about ¼ inch down from the top. Do the same on the second cylinder.
2. Write your secret code name on one cylinder. Give the other cylinder to your secret correspondent.

HOW TO SEND A MESSAGE

Remove the tack from the scytale. Stick the tack through the end of a ribbon, then reinsert it. Wrap the ribbon around the scytale in close spirals. Hold or tape the bottom end in place.
   Write your message in horizontal lines as shown. Release the bottom end of the ribbon, unwrap it, and remove the tack. Take the ribbon off the end of the tack and send it to your secret correspondent.

HOW TO DECIPHER A MESSAGE

You decipher a message the same way you send one. Although the message on the ribbon looks like a jumble of letters when you receive it unwound, as soon as you tack it to the matching scytale and rewrap it in close spirals, you will be able to read the horizontal lines of the message. The letters will fall neatly next to one another just as they were written.

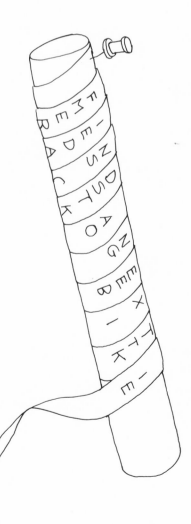

SIR JOHN, AN ENGLISH CRYPTOGRAPHER

In seventeenth-century England, there was a five-year period when Oliver Cromwell, a religious and political leader, overthrew the English monarchy and ruled the country. Many Royalists, or sympathizers of the deposed king, were imprisoned. One of those imprisoned in Colchester Castle was Sir John Trevanion.

Like other Royalists before him, Sir John would probably have been put to death but for a seemingly ordinary letter that he received in jail. The letter read:

Worthie Sir John: — Hope, that is ye beste comfort of ye afflicted, cannot much, I fear me, help you now. That I would saye to you, is this only: if ever I may be able to requite that I do owe you, stand not upon asking me. Tis not much that I can do: but what I can do, bee ye verie sure I wille. I knowe that, if dethe comes, if ordinary men fear it, it frights not you, accounting it for a high honour, to have such a rewarde of your loyalty. Pray yet that you may be spared this soe bitter cup. I fear not that you will grudge any sufferings; only if bie submission you can turn them away, tis the part of a wise man. Tell me, an if you can, to do for you anythinge that you wolde have done. The general goes back on Wednesday. Restinge your servant to command. — R.T.

But there was a hidden message within the simple note. If you read the letter as Sir John did—the third letter after every punctuation mark—you will learn that the PANEL AT EAST END OF CHAPEL SLIDES.

Sir John requested a private hour inside the prison chapel. But rather than spending his time in prayer, he escaped out the sliding panel. Secret communication saved his life.

Cipher Slide

Julius Caesar used a simple cipher to send his secret messages. He substituted each letter of the message with the third letter that followed it in the alphabet: *D* for *A*, *E* for *B*, and so on.

Substitution ciphers are easy to send and easy to decipher. That means they're not very safe for *top,* top secrets, but fun nevertheless. A handy device for generating substitution cipher alphabets is the Saint-Cyr slide, named after a French military academy where it was first used.

MATERIALS

Lightweight cardboard, 3 inches by 8½ inches
Ruler
Pencil
Matte knife or scissors
Heavy paper or lightweight cardboard, 1 inch by 15 inches
Pen and paper

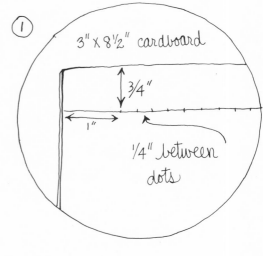

HOW TO MAKE A SLIDE

1. Hold the 3-inch piece of lightweight cardboard horizontally in front of you as shown. Measure ¾ inch down from the top and draw a line across. Beginning 1 inch from the left edge, mark off every ¼ inch with a dot on the line. Stop 1 inch from the right edge. There should be 26 dots altogether.
2. Above each dot, write in a letter of the alphabet. The letters should follow their regular sequence.
3. Measure ¼ inch below the first dot (below letter *A*) and ¼ inch to the left. Make one dot there and make another dot 1 inch below it. Use a matte knife or scissors to cut a slit between the two new dots. Do the same thing on the other side of the cardboard, below the last dot (below letter *Z* and ¼ inch to the right).

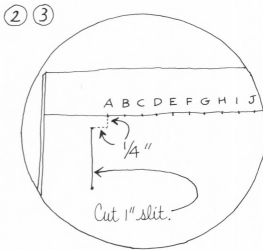

4. Place the 15-inch strip of paper horizontally in front of you. Measure ½ inch down from the top and draw a line across. Beginning 1 inch from the left, mark off every ¼ inch with a dot. Stop 1 inch from the right. There should be 52 dots altogether.
5. Above each dot on the strip of paper, write in a letter of the alphabet in regular sequence. It will take two alphabets to fill out the line.
6. Insert the strip in either slit of the cardboard so that the alphabet written on the paper slides under the one written on the cardboard.

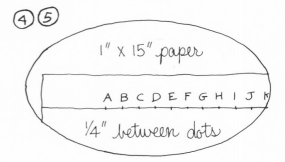

HOW TO SEND A MESSAGE

Assign a substitute letter code as Julius Caesar did. Slide the lower alphabet under the top one until the letter you want to substitute for *A* falls directly below *A*. Corresponding substitutes will fall under all the other letters on the top alphabet.

Prepare the text of a message. Rewrite the message in code, substituting the lower letters on the cipher slide for the corresponding ones in your message. Send the coded message to your secret correspondent.

HOW TO DECIPHER A MESSAGE

Decipher a message in substitute code in the same way that you send one—using a cipher slide to figure out the substitute letter pattern. But even with a slide, it's going to take a lot of sliding back and forth before you begin to see substitute letters form real words; that is, unless you take into consideration the frequency of certain letters, letter combinations, and words in the English language. Here's a chart that will help decipher a code with or without a cipher slide. It shows which letters, letter combinations, and words are used most frequently so that you can look for them first and save some time.

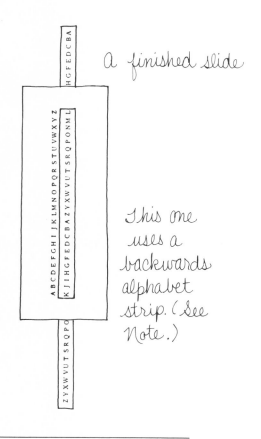

a finished slide

This one uses a backwards alphabet strip. (See Note.)

Order of frequency of—	Most frequent—
Single letters: E T O A N I R S H D L C W U M F Y G P B V K X Q J Z	Two-letter words: of to in it is be as at so we he by or on do if me my up an go no us am
Digraphs: th er on an re he in ed nd ha at en es of or nt ea ti to it st io le is ou ar as de rt ve	Three-letter words: the and for are but not you all any can had her was one our out day get has him his how man new now old see two way who boy did its let put say she too use
Most common doubles: ss ee tt ff ll mm oo	

Note: There are ways to make a substitute cipher more challenging. Rearrange the order of the alphabet on the paper strip. List the alphabet twice backwards, for example. Or, substitute 26 numbers or other symbols, recording them twice in whatever order you like on the paper strip. A substitute cipher with an alphabet that's out of normal sequence or composed of abstract symbols will take a iot more time to decipher.

Grilles

Grilles are like scytales (see Spartan Scytales, page 58) because they only work if two people have identical devices to decipher one another's messages. In this case, the device is a simple screen with a pattern of cutout windows. When the grille is superimposed over a jumble of letters or a seemingly ordinary message, a hidden message is revealed.

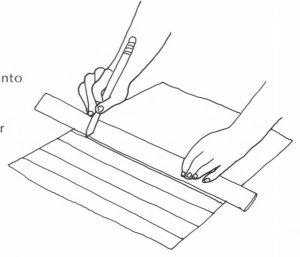

MATERIALS

Graph paper, 4 or 5 squares to the inch (You can make
    your own graph paper by ruling a plain sheet of paper into
    ¼-inch squares.)
Rubber cement
2 pieces of lightweight cardboard, such as bristol board or
    oaktag, cut to the size of the graph paper
Pencil
Matte knife
Plain paper, the same size as the graph paper
2 paper clips

HOW TO MAKE GRILLES

1. Brush rubber cement on the back of a sheet of graph paper and glue it to a piece of lightweight cardboard cut to the same size.
2. In light pencil, outline an area on the graph paper surface that is 4 or 5 square inches; for example, 25 squares by 25 squares if the graph paper has 5 squares to the inch.
3. Mark an X in 25 squares chosen at random inside the penciled area.
4. Use a matte knife to carefully cut out all the squares marked with an X.
5. Lay the grille over the second sheet of lightweight cardboard. Use a paper clip to hold the two together. Now trace the outside edges of the windows (the cutout squares) through the grille onto the cardboard underneath.
6. Remove the paper clip and separate the grille and cardboard. Cut out the squares in the cardboard. Now you have two identical grilles. Keep one and give the other to a friend.

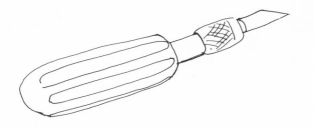

HOW TO SEND A MESSAGE

Place the sheet of plain paper behind the grille and use a paper clip to hold it in place. Write the letters of a message through the windows of the grille onto the plain paper. Write in the letters the same way as you read—from left to right, top to bottom.

Remove the clip and separate the grille and paper. Now write in other randomly chosen letters here and there among the ones included in the message. Place them above, below, to the sides, and in between the real letters of the message so that without the grille, the message cannot be read. Pass on the paper to the friend who has the other grille.

HOW TO DECIPHER A MESSAGE

Place the sheet of paper containing a secret message behind the grille. Use a paper clip to hold it in place. Read the letters from left to right that appear through the windows of the grille. They should reveal a secret message.

■ VARIATIONS

1. A square grille makes it possible to send a message that is four times as long as an ordinary grille. Make a square grille (for example, a grille that is cut to 8 inches by 8 inches). Divide the grille into four quadrants. Cut out all the windows from *one quadrant only*. Mark the top of the grille in some way so that you will know it is the top. To send a long message, place a sheet of paper under the grille, holding the grille with the top side up as you fill in the windows with the first part of your message. To continue the message, turn the grille 90 degrees clockwise (to the right) and once again fill in the windows. Turn the grille 90 degrees clockwise two more times, filling in the windows as before. The person receiving the message should read it the same way, starting with the grille top side up, then turning clockwise at 90 degree angles three times.

2. With your secret correspondent, decide beforehand to read from right to left, or from bottom right to top left, instead of the usual left to right, top to bottom. Or devise other ways to further obscure messages if you think that someone else has figured out your grille pattern. (How is this possible? If someone had intercepted two or more messages, that person may have discovered some regular intervals between the jumble of letters in your messages, intervals that produce letters that together make real words in both messages.)

Fill in with random letters.

Place grille over message to decipher.

Variation 1

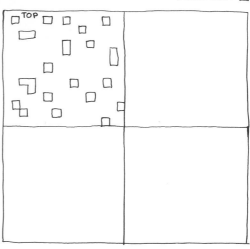

Poetry Grilles

Poetry grilles are a little impractical for serious cryptographers, but they're a challenge for poets who love devising clever ways to hide meanings or messages in their writing. The illustration shows how Emily Dickinson could have sent a message to a school friend by first incorporating the words of the message in a poem, then preparing a grille to reveal only those words.

Poetry grilles can be used to send secret messages in the text of poems by favorite writers or in new poems written just for the occasion.

MATERIALS

Original poem incorporating words of message
2 sheets of plain white paper
Typewriter or black felt-tip pen
Paper clip
Matte knife

HOW TO MAKE A POETRY GRILLE

1. On a plain sheet of paper, type or write out a poem incorporating the words of a hidden message. The words in the message must appear in the proper sequence; that is, in the same sequence in which they are to be read—left to right, top to bottom.
2. Place another sheet of white paper over the one that has the poem on it. Use a paper clip to hold it in place. The words on the bottom sheet should be visible through the top sheet of paper.
3. On the top sheet, outline the words in the poem that you want to include in the message. The word outlines should appear as rectangles.
4. Remove the paper clip and separate the sheets of paper. Cut out the rectangles on the top sheet to complete the grille.

HOW TO SEND AND DECIPHER A MESSAGE

Send both the typed sheet of poetry and the poetry grille. To decipher the message, place the poetry grille over the typed sheet of poetry and read the words that appear in the windows. Respond in kind: Select a favorite poem or write one that includes the words, in sequence, that you wish to send in reply.

Because I could not stop for Death
He kindly stopped for me—
The carriage held but just Ourselves—
And Immortality.

We slowly drove—He knew no haste
And I had put away
My labor and my leisure too,
For His Civility—

We passed the School, where Children strove
At Recess—in the Ring—
We passed the Fields of Grazing Grain—
We passed the Setting Sun—

Or rather—He passed Us—
The Dews drew quivering and chill—
For only Gossamer, my Gown—
My Tippet—only Tulle—

We paused before a House that seemed
A Swelling of the Ground—
The Roof was scarcely visible—
The Cornice—in the Ground—

Since then—'tis Centuries—and yet
Feels shorter than the Day
I first surmised the Horses' Heads
Were Toward Eternity—

Emily Dickinson

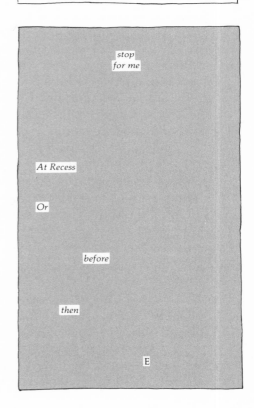

64

HOBO SIGNS

During the Great Depression in the 1930s, hoboes wandered around the countryside looking for food, clothing, and shelter. They had no jobs; instead they relied on generous people for free handouts. When people were not sympathetic, hoboes may have helped themselves to food from these people's gardens and clothing from their clotheslines. For this reason, hoboes were not very popular in many places.

As they traveled from town to town, hoboes left behind graffiti on walls, mailboxes, fences, poles, and trees. The graffiti was a form of secret picture writing known only to hoboes. It was a way to let the next hobo know the best places to go for food and shelter, and which places to avoid. Picture symbols were chalked in inconspicuous places where only another hobo would think to look for them. There were symbols that told a hobo he could sleep in a hayloft, or that if he told a certain lady a pitiful story she would give him food. There were signs warning a hobo that a mean dog was behind the fence, or that the folks in that particular town liked to beat up hoboes.

Safe campsight

Railroad

Food in exchange for work.

Keep going.

Police keep an eye on hoboes.

Police don't keep an eye on hoboes.

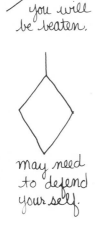

you will be beaten.

Mean dog

Okay to sleep in hayloft.

Gentleman

Lady

may need to defend yourself.

Telephone

Cares for sick hoboes

Tell a sad story.

Very good

Ghostwriter's Ink

Anyone who intercepts a message written in ghostwriter's ink won't even know there's a message to read! The only real risk in sending this invisible communication is that the receiver might throw it away by mistake. Therefore, messages in ghostwriter's ink are best sent and received by two friends in the know, or transmitted along with some visible instructions for reading them.

What is this marvelous stuff? One of two mysterious ingredients—lemon juice or milk! Although it dries clear, ghostwriter's ink can be made to reappear on a page as if by magic. Here's the secret: The heat of an incandescent light bulb will make lemon juice turn a brownish color. And shavings of graphite will blacken a sheet of paper everywhere except where it has been stained with milk, making the white message stand out. For those writers who might have to moonlight as magicians, a jar of either brew is useful to have around for magic tricks as well as invisible messages.

MATERIALS

Small jar with lid (for example, a small pimento jar, baby food jar, or sample-size jam jar)
Quill pen (see Quill Pen, page 7)
Paper for messages
Visible ink (see Berry Ink, page 9), ballpoint pen, or felt-tip pen

For Lemon Juice Recipe:
2 tablespoons of lemon juice
Lamp with ordinary incandescent light bulb

For Milk Recipe:
2 tablespoons of milk
Paring knife or penknife
Sharpened pencil

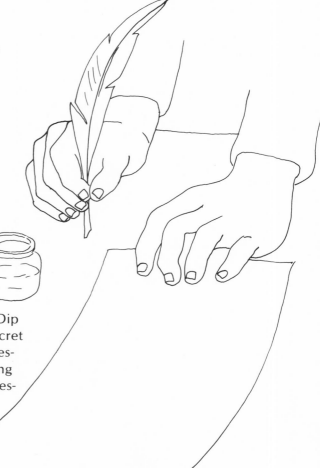

HOW TO SEND A MESSAGE

Put either the lemon juice or the milk into the small jar. Dip your quill pen into the invisible ink and write out your secret message on a piece of paper. Underneath the invisible message or on a separate page, write out directions for reading the message in ink that you can see (see how to read a message below). Allow the liquid to dry before you send the message.

Of course, there's no better time than Halloween to mail a friend a mysterious letter written in ghostwriter's ink. Just be sure to address the envelope in ordinary ink. If not, the post office will most likely give up the ghost and send the letter to the waste paper basket instead.

HOW TO READ A LEMON JUICE MESSAGE

Turn on the lamp. Hold the message you have received written in ghostwriter's ink up close to the light bulb. Within a few seconds, the invisible message will suddenly begin to appear as the heat of the burning light bulb turns the lemon juice brown.

HOW TO READ A MILK MESSAGE

Hold a sharpened pencil over the invisible message. Use a small, sharp knife to gently scrape off graphite onto the paper. Rub this powder over the paper lightly with your finger. The graphite will shade most of the paper lightly like a piece of artist's charcoal. But it will stick heavily to the fat in the dry milk. Therefore, the message written in milk will be darker and stand out clearly.

Lemon juice

Milk

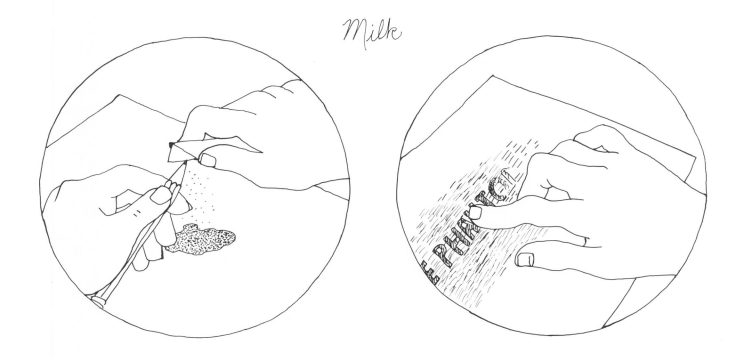

Rebus

A rebus is a form of riddle that uses pictures and symbols as substitutes for words, syllables, and sounds. It was a popular amusement printed in eighteenth- and nineteenth-century children's books and magazines that had titles such as *The Sphinx, The Puzzling Cap, A Pretty Riddle Book for Little Children,* and *The Whim Wham.* Some children's magazines today still include rebus puzzles. A rebus is not only fun to figure out, it's fun to compose and send to a friend to decipher. If it looks Egyptian at first, don't be surprised. Egyptian hieroglyphic writing is what inspired the rebus!

MATERIALS

Paper
Old magazines, newspapers, and catalogues
Scissors
Rubber cement
Colored felt-tip pens

DIRECTIONS

1. First write out on a sheet of paper the full text of a message, poem, nursery rhyme, or notable quote that you want to transcribe, or rewrite, in rebus form.
2. Now go back through the text, word by word, and figure out how you can use pictures, letters, and numbers to substitute for sounds, syllables, and words. Many examples are illustrated on this page.
3. On a fresh sheet of paper, begin to transcribe the text as a rebus. Find and cut out magazine pictures and other printed material to use as substitutes, then glue them in place. Draw pictures, letters, and numbers as well. A type catalogue will provide not only flamboyant letters and elegant numbers, but also little art symbols and designs. Use felt-tip pens to make the rebus colorful.
4. Either send the rebus to a friend to figure out, or hang it on the wall as a colorful poster.

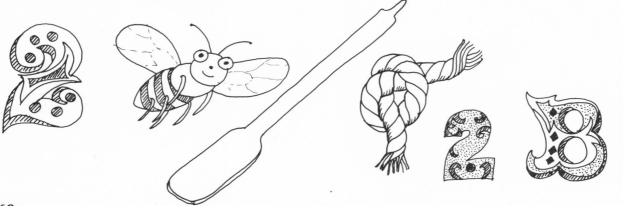

5

Writing for Fun

The projects featured in this chapter are just for fun. They show that writing can be a source of amusement or entertainment not connected with books or learning.

Writers are people who are in the business of creating original ideas. Much of the time, these ideas end up in such things as poems and short stories. But many of these same ideas can be applied to things that involve more active fun than reading. Some writers convert their ideas into exciting new games to play; others go on travel adventures and use writing as a camera to record their experiences; and still others combine writing with art to produce such frivolities as cartoons and comic strips.

Chapter Five includes seven projects in which writing serves not to fill a book, not to sit on display, not to communicate any particular idea, but just to provide a good time. Some activities are borrowed from writing amusements of the past. Others are favorites today. Many will change the way you think about writers and what they do. After all, how many people appreciate that behind every great board game, and behind every pack of trading cards, and behind every riddle-ridden treasure map is a good writer?

Thaumatrope Riddles

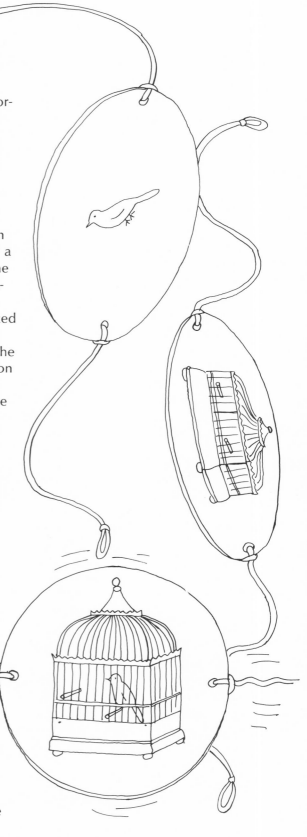

The thaumatrope, or "turning wonder," was a popular Victorian toy. It was a very simple device—a cardboard disk that was spun by twirling threads attached on either side of the disk between thumbs and index fingers. An incomplete picture was printed on each side. When the disk was spun, the viewer was able to see the complete picture all at once.

How is this possible? The retina of the eye retains an impression of an object a split second after the object has actually disappeared from view. This phenomenon is called an *after image*. If there are two picture parts, each on a side of a spinning disk, the viewer sees both parts at once because the disk is spinning so quickly that the viewer's eyes record continuous after images of each side.

The two picture parts on the thaumatrope disk were related not only by the way the images were superimposed when spinning, but by a riddle that the picture parts illustrated. The riddle question was printed on one side; the riddle answer, on the other along with the completing picture element.

When you're thinking up a riddle to put on a thaumatrope disk, keep in mind that riddles work because they set up a relationship between two otherwise unrelated objects or ideas. For example, the riddle, "Why is a book like a tree? They both have leaves!" compares a mechanically-made, lifeless object with one that is natural and quite alive. Two different meanings for the same word *leaves* is all that they have in common.

MATERIALS

3- to 4-inch piece of lightweight cardboard, such as bristol
   board or oaktag
Compass
Ruler
Scissors
Original riddle
White paper
Carbon paper
Felt-tip pens, at least 2 different colors
2 pieces of kite string or other sturdy thread, each
   6 inches long

DIRECTIONS

1. Set the compass for 2 or 3 inches in diameter. Insert the compass point in the cardboard and swing the pencil around to make a circle. Keep the compass at the same setting and make another circle on the white paper.

2. Line up the edge of the ruler with the center point of the cardboard circle. Draw a light line across the diameter of the circle. From the edge of the circle, measure in ⅛ inch along this line and make a mark. With the point of the compass, punch a small hole at each mark to put the string through. Do the same for the paper circle.
3. Cut out the cardboard circle.
4. Lay the paper circle faceup so that the line between the two string holes is horizontal. Inside the paper circle, draw a picture that incorporates the two unrelated objects or ideas that are the subjects of your riddle. Make sure both elements are included clearly in the design.
5. Cut out the paper circle. Cut out a piece of carbon paper that is about the same size as the circle. Glue the *back side* of the carbon paper (the side that does not print) to the back side of the circle. It doesn't matter if the carbon paper sticks out a little all around. Punch through the string holes again with the point of the compass so that the carbon paper is punched through as well.
6. Lay the paper circle on top of the cardboard disk. Move it until the string holes match up on either side. Use a pencil to retrace the *first* element of the design (see side 1 in the illustration) so that it is transferred by the carbon backing to the cardboard disk.
7. Remove the paper circle. Flip the cardboard disk over—not sideways, but bottom over top—to the other side. (You are turning the disk over the same way it will revolve on the strings.) The picture part on the other side should be facedown and upside down.
8. Once again, lay the paper circle on top of the cardboard disk and match up the string holes on either side. Now trace the *second* element of the design (see side 2 of the illustration) so that it is transferred onto the cardboard disk.
9. Remove the paper circle and color in the picture parts on both sides of the disk, using different colored pens for each side.
10. In small print, write the riddle question on side 1 of the disk, the side with the first element of the design. Write the answer to the riddle on side 2.
11. Insert a piece of string through each string hole in the disk. Knot one end of each string so that it cannot slip back out of its hole.
12. Pick up the disk by the strings so that each string is held between the thumb and index finger of each hand. Twirl the strings back and forth between your fingers to make the disk spin. You should be able to see the complete riddle picture at once.

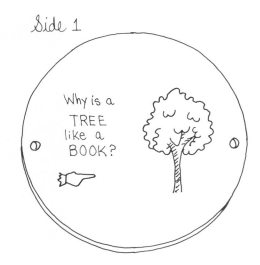

Side 1

Why is a TREE like a BOOK?

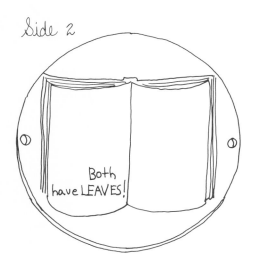

Side 2

Both have LEAVES!

Twirl strings to spin disk.

Why is a TREE like a BOOK? Both have LEAVES!

Writer's Trading Cards

At the turn of the century, a very popular advertising gimmick was to enclose trading cards inside packaged goods. Makers of tobacco products and breakfast foods enclosed pretty colorprinted cards containing pictures of, and stories about, people, places, plants, or animals. A package of cigarettes, for example, might have inside a card with a picture of a flowering plant on one side and a botanical description on the other. People were encouraged to continue buying cigarettes until they had collected a complete herbal of flowering plants.

The same advertising gimmick is used today. As any baseball fan knows, inside packages of certain kinds of bubble gum is a baseball trading card. There are trading cards for football fans, too. Why not create a set of writer's trading cards for fans of great writers?

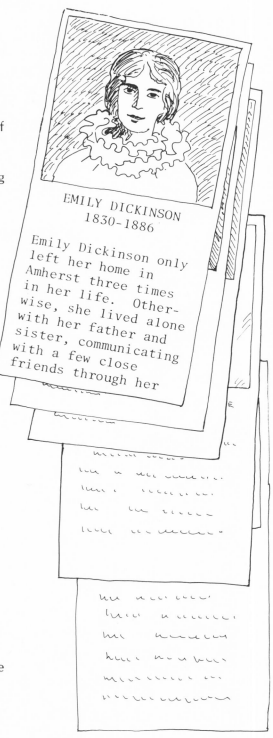

EMILY DICKINSON
1830–1886

Emily Dickinson only left her home in Amherst three times in her life. Otherwise, she lived alone with her father and sister, communicating with a few close friends through her

MATERIALS

Pictures of famous writers (cut from newspaper reviews, magazine interviews, advertisements, or photocopies of portraits in books)
Biographies of famous writers
Scissors
Card stock (65- or 80-pound paper) cut to a uniform size; for example, 2 inches by 4 inches
Rubber cement
Typewriter or pen
Transparent contact paper
Cutting board or other scratchable work surface
Matte knife
Metal ruler or other metal straightedge

DIRECTIONS

1. Decide on a category of famous writers; for example, modern poets, writers of classics, famous novelists, great playwrights, popular song writers, women writers, or Afro-American writers. Come up with a list of names that can be included in your category. Research those writers in the library.
2. Make a trading card for each writer. First, cut out a small portrait or photo of the writer and glue it down at the top of the card. Then, write or type in a very short biography, including the year of birth and (if applicable) year of death, nationality, people or events which influenced the writer's work, and a list of publications. Unless the

biography is written in short phrases, typewriter lettering will probably be too large for the card, so have a pen ready. (Remember, you can use the back of the card, too.)

3. Cut out two pieces of transparent contact paper a little larger than the card all around. Remove the paper backing on one piece and lay it down with the sticky side up. Position the card on top of the contact paper so that all parts of the card are on the plastic. Remove the backing on the second piece of contact paper. Position this piece on top of the first piece so that the card is completely covered by and sandwiched in between the two sticky surfaces. This process of sealing the card in a clear, protective covering is called *laminating*.

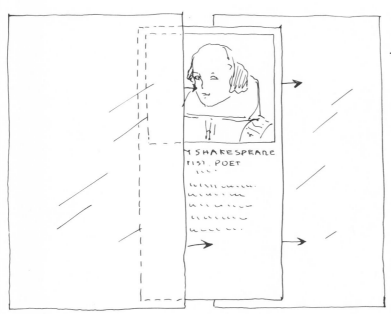

Transparent contact paper.

LANGSTON HUGHES
1902-1967

Langston Hughes was a poet who wrote about the desperate lives of black people in Harlem and other American ghettos. He also wrote novels, plays, and several collections of short stories. His poems are written in free verse. Although they

4. Place the laminated construction on top of a cutting board or a work surface you don't mind scratching. Lay a metal ruler or straightedge along one side of the sealed card. Run the blade of a matte knife along the metal edge two times—first to score the plastic, then to cut through it. Discard the piece cut off. Do the same on the other three sides of the card so that all the excess plastic is trimmed away. Scissors may also be used.

5. Follow steps 2 through 4 to make a laminated card for each writer. If you are a member of a literary circle (a group of writer friends), encourage fellow writers to make similar sets. Then, when you get together to read each other's latest works, trade cards as well as criticism.

Adventure Board Game

Writers of science fiction, detective mysteries, fantasy, or other adventure stories all have in their fiction the makings of a great game.

Adventure board games are like stories with multiple plots. The players are the characters. The dice a player throws, the spaces a player lands on, and the instructions a player receives on game cards all determine the fate of the character. The best part is that every ending is a surprise—even to the author of the game who doesn't know which character will come out ahead until the game is played.

This project involves both writing and crafting. The game equipment is easy enough to make; writing the text for the cards and board spaces is the real creative challenge.

MATERIALS

Shirt box
2 pieces of cardboard, ½ inch less on each side than the measurements of the shirt box (Corrugated cardboard panels from cardboard boxes are okay.)
Paper for game board, cut to the same length as the cardboard and twice the width of 1 piece plus ¼ inch (Large, "parent size" sheets are available in art or graphic art supply stores.)
Cellophane tape
Cloth tape, 1 inch wide
Pencil
Ruler
Colored felt-tip pens
Rubber cement
Scissors
Plain wrapping paper
Decorative borders and illustrations
40 pieces of card stock (65- or 80-pound paper), cut to playing card size
Transparent contact paper (available in the housewares section of most department stores)
Self-hardening modeling clay
Poster paints and a paintbrush
Acrylic sealer in spray can
Pair of dice (available at game stores)

Decorate your game box →

74

HOW TO PLAN A GAME

1. Choose an adventure theme—for example, space exploration or an enchanted forest. Assign a mission that must be accomplished before a player can win. In a game about space exploration, the mission might be to establish three space colonies before returning home to the space station. In a game about an enchanted forest, the mission might be simply to find your way out.

2. On a sheet of card stock or paper, write out directions and rules for playing the game. The qualifications for winning may be very simple or somewhat complicated. For example, the winner might simply be the first player to go completely around the board. Or, in a more complicated game, the winner might be the first player to accomplish a certain number of tasks and get to the FINISH space safely. This might require circling the board several times before succeeding.

HOW TO MAKE THE GAME BOARD AND BOX

1. Place the two pieces of cardboard side by side, with a ¼-inch space between them as shown. Lay two small pieces of cellophane tape across them to hold them in this position.

2. Bind the boards together with a long strip of cloth tape, laying the tape down along first one side, then back up the other as shown. Now you have one large game board. Fold it in half along the taped seam and crease the fold well. Leave the board folded until you get to step 8.

3. With a ruler and pencil, design the game sheet on the large piece of paper. Draw in blocks, or spaces, around the sides of the sheet. Designate one corner block as the START and FINISH space. In the center of the sheet, indicate a place for a pile of ADVENTURE CARDS and another for a pile of MISADVENTURE CARDS.

4. Write the text for the three remaining corner spaces first. Make these three spaces obstacles—situations which will delay the players on their trip around the board.

5. Mark at least a third of the spaces ADVENTURE or MISADVENTURE (the same number of each). When players land on these spaces, they will draw a card from the respective piles. Mark one or two spaces GO TO NEXT ADVENTURE SPACE; another one or two spaces GO TO NEXT MISADVENTURE SPACE.

6. Mark the remaining spaces with the names of places, keeping to your adventure theme. For example, places in an enchanted forest might include Fairy Circle, Cave of Demons, and Wizard's Hollow. Place names with a science fiction theme are included in the sample game board shown here.

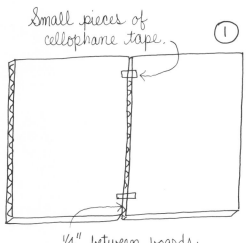

Small pieces of cellophane tape.

①

¼" between boards

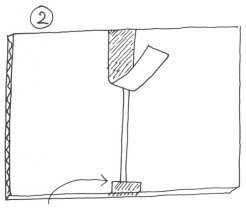

②

Bind boards together with cloth tape.

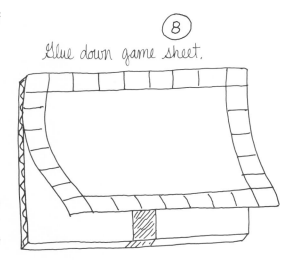

⑧

Glue down game sheet.

7. Illustrate and color in all the spaces on the game sheet.
8. Reopen the board. Brush rubber cement on the back of the game sheet. Glue the sheet faceup on the game board. Then refold the board so that the game sheet is on the inside.
9. Examine the shirt box. If it has writing on it, either paint it or cover it with plain wrapping paper. Decorate the top of the lid with the title of the game, borders, and illustrations. Brush rubber cement on the back of the sheet of directions you wrote in step 2 of How to Plan a Game and paste it on the inside of the lid.

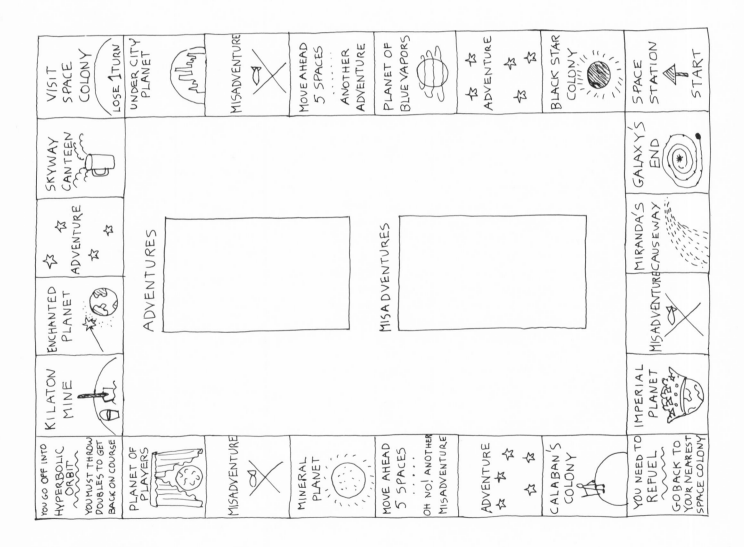

HOW TO MAKE GAME CARDS AND PLAYING PIECES

1. Count out 20 cards. On one side of each card, print the word ADVENTURE. On the remaining 20 cards, print the word MISADVENTURE.

2. Begin with the ADVENTURE cards. On the blank side of each card, write out the text of an adventure that will allow a player to advance more quickly on the board (for example, move ahead a certain number of spaces, or take an extra turn). Or write an adventure that will give the player an opportunity to achieve or gain something necessary for winning. (See the examples.) These adventures should be in keeping with the game theme. Some of them should relate to specific places on the board, places that will help players accomplish their missions. If there is room on the cards, illustrate them.

3. On the back of each MISADVENTURE card, write out the text of an adventure that creates a setback for the player—for example, the player might have to backtrack a certain number of spaces, lose a turn, or give up something that has been achieved or gained along the way.

4. Follow steps 3 and 4 in Writer's Trading Cards (page 72) to laminate the ADVENTURE and MISADVENTURE cards. This will keep the cards from becoming bent or torn from constant handling.

5. Mold four small, flat-bottomed playing pieces out of clay. After the clay is hardened, paint the pieces. When the paint is dry, spray on a coat of acrylic sealer. Each piece must be different in some way, either a different shape or a different color, so that players will be able to tell them apart. The pieces should be small enough so that two will sit comfortably on any one space.

Invite some friends or family to try out your game. Have each player select a playing piece and roll the pair of dice. The player who rolls the highest number goes first. When you are ready to put away the game, place the playing pieces, cards, and dice in little plastic bags. Fold the game board in half and lay it inside the bottom of the shirt box. Lay the bags on top. Put on the lid and store the game on a shelf or other flat surface.

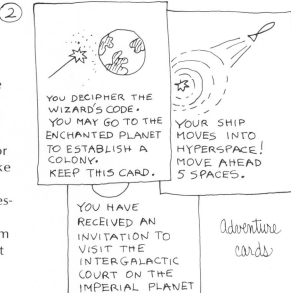

② YOU DECIPHER THE WIZARD'S CODE. YOU MAY GO TO THE ENCHANTED PLANET TO ESTABLISH A COLONY. KEEP THIS CARD.

YOUR SHIP MOVES INTO HYPERSPACE! MOVE AHEAD 5 SPACES.

YOU HAVE RECEIVED AN INVITATION TO VISIT THE INTERGALACTIC COURT ON THE IMPERIAL PLANET

adventure cards

Misadventure cards

③ SUPER NOVA EXPLOSION! CHANGE YOUR COURSE. GO BACK 3 SPACES

YOUR SHIP IS BOMBARDED BY A METEORITE SHOWER! REPAIR DAMAGE TO YOUR SHIP WHERE YOU HAVE BEEN STRUCK. LOSE 1 TURN.

YOU ENTER A BLACK HOLE! RETURN TO SPACE STATION. YOU MUST GIVE UP ANY COLONIES YOU HAVE ESTABLISHED.

OF FUEL CK E STATION 2 TURNS

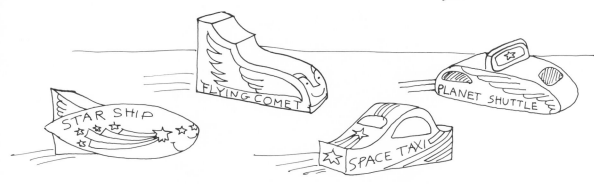

STAR SHIP

FLYING COMET

SPACE TAXI

PLANET SHUTTLE

77

Phototoons

Phototoons are comic strips that feature photos of real people instead of cartoon caricatures. They are perfect for writers who can't draw well. The cast of characters can include friends, classmates, family members, neighbors, pets, and anyone else who happens to be on scene during the shooting. The writer is responsible for creating a script, directing the cast, snapping the photos, selecting and editing the final *frames* (the boxed units of action in the comic strip story), and writing lines of dialogue inside voice balloons.

Like an ordinary comic strip, a phototoon can be funny, suspenseful, or dramatic. It might recount the adventures of supersleuths or superheroes, or make fun of ordinary people and day-to-day events. No matter what they're about, phototoons are as much fun to make as they are to share afterwards.

MATERIALS

Camera
1 or 2 rolls of black-and-white or color film (enough for at least 2 shots of every frame)
Script or plot outline
Costumes and props if necessary
Plain paper
Black felt-tip pen
Scissors
Old magazines (optional—see step 6)
Rubber cement

DIRECTIONS

1. Write a script for the phototoon and dialogue to go inside the speech balloons. Decide how you want the scenes to look.
2. Read the script, or the outline of the plot, to the members of the cast. Then direct the cast for shooting the first frame of your phototoon comic strip. Provide costumes or props if necessary. Explain where you want the characters to be, how you want them to interact with each other, and what they ought to be thinking so that certain expressions will appear on their faces. What they ought to be thinking are the lines of dialogue that you will write inside voice balloons later on. Take at least two snapshots of each frame.

3. Continue reading the script, directing, and photographing each scene until you have completed all the frames for the strip.

4. Have the film developed. When the prints are returned to you, sort them out into scenes and select the best photo for each. Each photo will appear in one frame of the comic strip.

5. On a sheet of plain paper, lay out the photos in sequence. Space them far enough apart so that you can draw in voice balloons. You may need several sheets for the entire phototoon, depending on the length of the plot and the number of frames you photographed. If you like, you can arrange photos side by side in horizontal rows and blacken in the lines of each frame. Or you can arrange the photos wherever they look best and number them so that the reader can follow the sequence.

6. Some photos will need editing. In other words, you may want to cut away parts of the photo that you don't need or that distract from the main subject in the frame. Cut around characters or objects carefully so that you leave the important material intact. If you need some special effects—for example, if your superheroine is to be attacked by a fruit fly the size of a helicopter—cut out objects appearing in magazine photos that have been photographed at different distances, then place them in your own photo frames where they will appear oversized or undersized.

7. Reposition all the edited photos. Brush rubber cement on the backs and glue the photos in place on the sheets of paper.

8. Draw voice balloons or thought balloons coming out of characters' mouths or floating about their heads like clouds. Write lines of dialogue or thoughts inside the balloons.

9. Design a title page or cover for the phototoon. Place this sheet on top of the others and staple the whole batch. Or, for a more fancy effect, try making a laced binding (see Autograph Album, page 36) or a stitched binding (see Simple Stitched Book, page 30).

Wanda the Wizard

by Anondo and Indrani Stangl

Post Card Travelogue

Most writers like to keep notes on their travel adventures. In the nineteenth century, many people, including Queen Victoria of England, published these journals, or travelogues, to share with others who were about to set out on voyages and visits of their own. Some travelogues included sketches of places and people a traveler encountered along the way.

An up-to-date version of such a journal is the post card travelogue. It's an exciting and colorful record of a traveler's experiences on the road that is waiting safe at home when he or she returns.

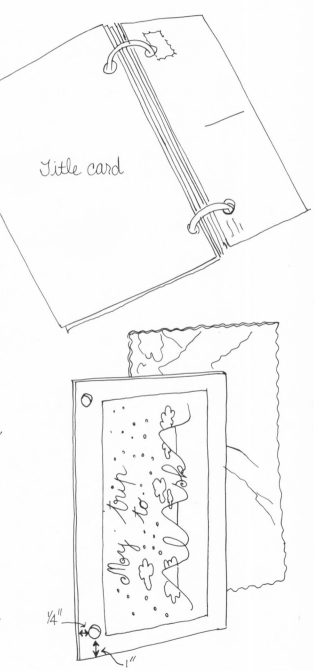

MATERIALS

Picture post cards from your voyages and visits away
   from home
Blank card, 3½ inches by 5½ inches
Felt-tip pens
Hole punch
2 metal bindery rings (available in stationery stores)

DIRECTIONS

1. During your travels, purchase picture post cards of places you have seen and would like to remember. On the back of each card, write in the date and a description of your experiences at the place pictured on the card. Then, either address and send the card to yourself at home, or send it to a friend or relative with a postscript asking that person to save it for you.
2. When you return from your travels, assemble all the picture post cards in the order you wrote them.
3. On a blank card, write a title, such as "My Trip to Alaska." Decorate the title card.
4. Punch a hole in the title card, 1 inch from the left side of the card and ¼ inch from the top. Punch a second hole in the same position on the right side of the card.
5. Use the title card as a template. Position it on each post card and punch through both holes into the card below.
6. Open the bindery rings. In reverse order, slip each card, picture side faceup, through the holes onto the bindery rings. Slip the title card on last, then close the rings.
7. Add to the travelogue after each trip to a new place or each visit to an old friend or family. Design a title card for each set of post cards. From time to time, flip through your post card travelogue as you would a photograph album or a journal, and remember your adventures and unusual experiences away from home.

Treasure Map

The idea of hidden treasure—the gleam of gold and the dazzle of jewels—has enticed people for as long as there has been anything valuable to hide. Stealing treasure was the favorite occupation of seventeenth-century pirates whose sunken ships and buried troves are still the quest of treasure hunters today.

Some treasure hunters are lucky enough to have directions for finding a buried trove in the form of a treasure map. Treasure maps are usually made by the treasure hiders as reminders to themselves of where to find the treasure when they want to dig it up or as directions to a close friend or partner. The maps are as cryptic as possible so that if the wrong people somehow get the map, they won't be able to understand it. So, a treasure map is often like a picture mystery that the treasure hunter must solve. The clues—both words and pictures—are in riddles. The treasure hunter must solve these riddles in order to discover the exact location of the hidden treasure.

Fortunately, going on a treasure hunt is so much fun that it seems worthwhile even if the "treasure" is considerably less valuable than gold or jewels. And burying a treasure and mapping its location is as fun as participating in the hunt itself. But it takes a good riddle writer to set up a treasure hunt that is truly challenging. The occasion for a treasure hunt might be Easter (an egg hunt), Passover (the ritual of hiding matzoh), or a party (a searching game for hidden prizes). But you don't need an excuse to have one—just something to hide.

MATERIALS

Treasure object(s)
Paper
Colored felt-tip pens

DIRECTIONS

1. Hide your treasure. Choose a place where a treasure hunter might not think to look. If you plan to bury it in the ground, make sure it is a good distance from the garden to avoid digging up next spring's flower bulbs by mistake.

2. In one corner of a piece of paper, mark the four compass points. This is especially important if you are going to lead the treasure hunter in a roundabout way to the treasure. Choose a starting point and either label it or write a riddle whose solution will provide the starting position.

3. Continue mapping out the course the treasure hunter must follow. Identify landmarks by means of riddles or riddle pictures. For example, if the hunter is to go to the fork in the path, draw in a picture of the eating utensil and let the hunter guess its meaning. Or write a riddle like this:

My first is first's also	(F)
My second needs filling	(O)
My third is the end of four	(R)
My last one starts killing	(K)

   If the hunter is to take a right, you might indicate that with an arrow, or you might write, "I salute you!" (One salutes with the right hand.)

4. When you have finished your map, present it to a friend or a brother or sister. Or leave it in a place where someone is very likely to come upon it; for example, taped to a mirror, or resting on a pillow. If the map is for an Easter egg hunt, it could be taped on the inside lid of an empty egg carton in which the hunter can store the chocolate or hard-boiled treasures.

I'll replace your pearl with silver
When my gold ship sails tonight.
Look underneath a white bird's breast
When my ship is out of sight.

Map for the Easter Egg Hunt

MASQUERADE, *A TREASURE BOOK*

Somewhere in Britain, a real treasure was buried in a ceramic container bearing the inscription:

I am the keeper of the Jewel of
MASQUERADE
which lies safe inside me
for you or Eternity.

The treasure (or Jewel) is a golden hare, adorned with precious stones and glazed earthenware. The exact location of the Jewel is given in Masquerade (New York: Schocken Books, 1980), a fantasy written and illustrated by Kit Williams, the artist who made and buried the golden treasure. But a reader must find the Jewel by solving the many riddle-clues hidden in the text and illustrations.

Masquerade is the story of Jack Hare, a messenger who must travel through earth, air, fire, and water to deliver the Jewel as a gift of love from the Moon to the Sun. Jack Hare has many adventures and misadventures along the way, and only at the end discovers that the Jewel is lost. Where it was lost and where the treasure was buried is the final riddle in this unusual literary treasure map.

Mr. Williams said that the riddle could be solved by a ten-year-old just as easily as a college graduate. He assured his readers that no knowledge of British geography is necessary to guess the location of the buried treasure. Although the Jewel has since been found, readers continue to enjoy reading and examining Mr. Williams' book for clues to where it was once hidden. Perhaps this treasure book will inspire others like it.

Writing for Profit

A KIDS' GUIDE TO PLACES THAT PUBLISH

Publishers of magazines and books *for* kids are often very happy to consider writing submitted *by* kids. Most of these publishers will send a copy of their writing guidelines to writers who send a self-addressed, stamped envelope. It's also a good idea to take a look at other publications to get an idea of what a publisher might look for in a manuscript. If you do send your writing to a publisher, be sure to include your name, address, age, and school year in a short letter of introduction along with your work. Send another self-addressed, stamped envelope to have your manuscript returned if the publisher decides not to publish it.

Cricket

P.O. Box 100
LaSalle, Illinois 61301

Cricket is a monthly magazine for kids, ages 6–12. It sponsors many poetry, story, and drawing contests, and publishes the winning entries.

Ebony Jr.!

Johnson Publishing Company
820 S. Michigan Avenue
Chicago, Illinois 60605

Ebony Jr.! is a monthly magazine that publishes nonfiction, fiction, and poetry about black kids.

Jack and Jill

Children's Health Publications
P.O. Box 567B
Indianapolis, Indiana 46206

Jack and Jill is a magazine for kids, ages 8–12. It is published nine times a year. A regular feature called "Our Readers Write" accepts poetry on health subjects, such as exercise, safety, and nutrition. *Jack and Jill* also publishes original riddles submitted by readers, and will provide a list of pen pals if you send 50 cents to Pen Pals at the address above.

Plays: The Dramatic Magazine for Young People

Plays, Inc.
8 Arlington Street
Boston, Massachusetts 02116

Plays publishes a number of short plays and skits every month for kids in primary, middle, and senior high grades. Many of these plays are also published in book collections.

Ranger Rick's Nature Magazine

1412 16th Street, NW
Washington, D.C. 20036

Ranger Rick is published monthly for kids, ages 4–12. It accepts poetry, "Knock-Knock" jokes, and stories on nature subjects.

Stone Soup

P.O. Box 83
Santa Cruz, California 95063

Stone Soup is a literary journal for kids that is published five times a year. It accepts stories, drawings, and some poetry. It is the most professional kids' publication around.

Old-Style Alphabets

AABCDEFGHIJ
KKLMMNNOP
QRSTUUVWXYZ

ABCDEF abcdefg
GHIJKLM hijklmn
NOPQRST opqrstu
UVWXYZ vwxyz

ABCDEFGHIJKLM
NOPQRSTUVWXYZ

Old-Style Alphabets

ABCDEFG
HIJKLM
NOPQRSF
UVWXYZ

abcdefghijklmn
opqrstuvwxyz

ABCDEFGHI
JKLMNOPQR
STUVWXYZ
abcdefghijk
lmnopqrst
uvwxyz

Stencil Alphabets

ABCDEF
GHIJKL
MNOPQ
RSTUVW
XYZ

ABCDEFGH
IJKLMNOPQRS
TUVWXYZ&

Printer's Devices and Dingbats

Monograms and Elegant Initials

Border Art

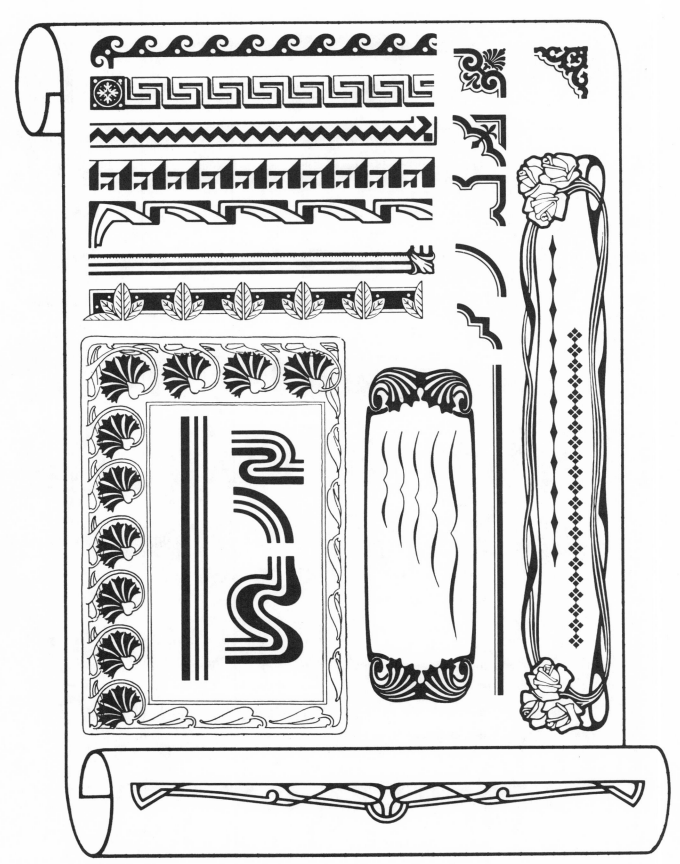

Calligraphic Alphabets

ABCDEFGHIJ
KLMNOPQR
STUVWXYZ
&.,abcdefghijklm
nopqrstuvwxyz
1234567890

THE QUICK BROWN
FOX JUMPS OVER
THE LAZY DOG

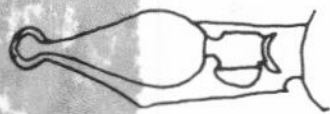

Use a round, flat point for this alphabet.

91

Calligraphic Alphabets

A B C D E F G H I
J K L M N O P R
Q T S U V W X Y
Z a b b c d e f g h h i j k k l l
m n o p q r s t u v w x y y z

A B C D E F G H I J K L M N
O P Q R S T U V W X Y Z a b c d
e f g h i j k l m n o p q r s t u v w x y z